RISK
AND
CRISIS
MANAGEMENT

101 Cases

Revised Edition

RISK

—AND—

CRISIS

MANAGEMENT

Revised Edition

Akira Ishikawa
Aoyama Gakuin University, Japan

Atsushi Tsujimoto
The University of Tokyo, Japan

World Scientific

NEW JERSEY · LONDON · SINGAPORE · BEIJING · SHANGHAI · HONG KONG · TAIPEI · CHENNAI

Published by

World Scientific Publishing Co. Pte. Ltd.

5 Toh Tuck Link, Singapore 596224

USA office: 27 Warren Street, Suite 401–402, Hackensack, NJ 07601

UK office: 57 Shelton Street, Covent Garden, London WC2H 9HE

British Library Cataloguing-in-Publication Data
A catalogue record for this book is available from the British Library.

RISK AND CRISIS MANAGEMENT
101 Cases
(Revised Edition)

ISBN-13 978-981-4273-89-3
ISBN-10 981-4273-89-9

Typeset by Stallion Press
Email: enquiries@stallionpress.com

Printed in Singapore by B & Jo Enterprise Pte Ltd

Foreword

Large-scale earthquakes have been occurring with noticeable frequency recently. While we were still in the process of recovering from the nightmares of the Great Hanshin-Awaji Earthquake and the Chuetsu Earthquake of Niigata Prefecture in Japan, the Sumatra Earthquake and a major tremor in the Indo-Pakistani border region caught us. As of this writing (November 9, 2005), more than 87,000 people have fallen victim to the Indo-Pakistani border tremor. The Sumatra Earthquake was immediately followed by a tremendously powerful tsunami, making it impossible to do anything much about the after effects of the quake itself. Much time has gone into damage estimation and restoration of order in the affected areas.

Disasters have not been limited to earthquakes. Damage brought on by hurricanes in various parts of the world, especially the hurricane miseries experienced in the United States, were of unprecedented scale. Who could have predicted that New Orleans, a major metropolis in the south of the United States, would undergo damage so destructive that it would completely paralyze the city? Reportedly, much of the U.S. defense effort had been redirected toward terrorism deterrence and prevention, with relevant agencies and related organizations reconfigured in the aftermath of the September 11, 2001 terrorist attacks in the United States. Subsequent terrorist bomb attacks in London and Madrid have resulted in diminished attention paid to the prevention of exposure to damage caused by hurricane, rain and flood.

The Japanese Central Disaster Prevention Conference has announced that there is a 70 percent chance that a magnitude 7-class major earthquake will hit the National Capital region at some point during the next three decades. If an earthquake of such magnitude hits the northern portion of Tokyo Bay, the number of dead and wounded is estimated to exceed 11,000. The cause of death for 90 percent of the well over 100,000 victims and missing persons of the 1923 Great Kanto Earthquake was attributed to fire exposure, at the time. However, the current mainstream view now estimates that about 5,500 died by fire, and that the rest were crushed to death within seconds of the sudden attack of the violent tremor. These are all cases that would be covered by risk and crisis management.

Risk and crisis management addresses the protection of people's lives and assets. No problem is so simple and easy that it can be addressed in a single, sweeping stroke. To the extent that society must unconditionally put it at the top of the priority list precisely because it concerns the lives of people, we are dealing here with an issue of intellectual dimensions.

As the reader scans the text for these keywords, he or she will be able to grasp what components should go into an emergency scenario. Other supplementary issues to be addressed have been presented at the end of the volume in the form of questions to test the reader's understanding in the pertinent context. The reader is urged, after having studied the book, to try the exercise to confirm his or her understanding before taking on the recommended preparations.

The essential purpose of this book lies in urging the reader to take immediate action after having grasped its content and gained an in-depth understanding of the concepts. The essence of study does not end with merely understanding, but must include the creative projection of scenario planning and simulation drills. The completion of such a process would, as a matter of course, be predicated on the preparation of necessary materials and an unrelenting pursuit of practice makes perfect.

Disaster prevention centers are to be found in every region all over Japan (in Tokyo: at Honjo, Ikebukuro, Tachikawa and elsewhere). To visit one of these centers and actually experience a simulated quake and its management — via fire-fighting, movement through smoke, first aid and other life-saving techniques, etc. — will prove to be of immense value.

Among other components of risk and crisis management, anti-disaster preparedness has deep, immeasurable implications and can never be regarded as complete, no matter how confident one may feel in terms of having done everything possible. Everyone must be keenly mindful at all times that the ultimate self-help can only come in the moment of truth based on his or her commitment to constant planning and preparation.

* * *

This is a revised and enlarged edition of *Survival — Simulation of Risk and Crisis Management 69*, which was published in 1999. It incorporates additions and corrections made to reflect what we have learned about the characteristics of the natural and man-made disasters that have occurred since the first edition went to press. It also includes the study of new measures taken to overcome disasters since that time. Accordingly, additional keywords and illustrative examples have been incorporated.

In the preparation of this edition, the author has been blessed with very enthusiastic support from President Mamoru Miura of Shumpusha Publishing, as well as his project manager Toshinobu Nagata, and dedicated staff. The author wishes to acknowledge his deepest gratitude for this assistance.

Akira Ishikawa
November 2005

Contents

RISK AND CRISIS MANAGEMENT   65
FOR DAILY LIFE: CASES 28–62

Risk and Crisis Management for Natural Disasters: Cases 1–27

Case 1

How the Internet is a Useful Crisis Management Tool

To improve contingency planning (CP) or crisis management, it is necessary to develop relevant infrastructure, particularly communication networks.

Immediately after the Great Hanshin-Awaji Earthquake in 1995, the mass media provided round-the-clock news coverage of the disaster site on television and radio. Also, the names of victims, particularly of those who were confirmed dead, were continuously updated. However, information on survivors, such as their location, contact phone numbers and condition, was scarce although it was a matter of great concern for families, relatives and friends.

This is where the **Internet** came to play an important role.

On the evening of 17 January, only half a day after the earthquake, a bulletin board system (BBS) was set up on the Internet to exclusively provide seismic information. The next day, an online service provider, ATSON Inc., which operated ASAHI Net, began posting the names of people who had died. By 23 January, major online service providers, Nifty-Serve and PC-VAN, had each posted about 400 references of earthquake-related information on their websites (*Nikkei Industry News*, **24 January 1995**).

Among these references were many postings on the status of individual survivors, which tended to not be well-covered by the traditional mass media. Thus, personal computer networks demonstrated their superiority in transmitting and receiving information under circumstances where cellular and fixed-line telephones were disabled.

Unfortunately, it is also true that those without computers or those unfamiliar with personal computer communication were not able to send or receive information.

To ensure information access in future emergencies, it is critical to establish **wireless communication** networks connected to portable terminal devices.

KEY POINT

In managing a crisis, technology needs to be tapped.

Recommendations

In disaster-prone areas:

1. Wireless network devices must be made affordable and widely available;
2. Personal computer networks must be further enhanced;
3. The function of providing survivor information, such as their condition, contact numbers and evacuation location should be improved.

Case 2

How Communication Technology Must Be Harnessed in an Emergency

In the event of a major earthquake, we are likely to depend on leased or private fixed-line telephone services, which, in reality, are not reliable. Unless we can access other means of communication, CP (contingency plans) will fail.

The more urgent an emergency, the more important it is to make full use of all available public and private telephone lines. However, at the time of the Great Hanshin-Awaji Earthquake, more than 300,000 private telephone lines and 4,000 business leased lines were disabled. Further, over 145 mobile communication bases were damaged (*Yomiuri Shimbun*, **30 May 1995**).

On top of the massive system breakdown, the number of attempted telephone calls from Tokyo to the disaster area exceeded the usual volume by 50 times, which overwhelmed the already limited phone lines. Additionally, the number of available telephone lines was restricted to 10 percent. Thus, you were lucky if one out of 10 attempted calls you made got through.

This is where the Internet, although unanticipated to the Internet originating, came to demonstrate its effectiveness as a communication tool. There were 600,000 discrete access events superiorly from 50 countries around the world by the end of February in 1995.

Nifty-Serve received about a million accesses from inside Japan by the end of January, 1995. Assuming each visitor spent three minutes on average, it could be calculated that as many as 70,000 people used the Internet services.

Thus, the personal computer proved to be a very effective tool for obtaining information about earthquake victims. Based on past disaster procedures, authorities would post many fliers near public telephones, informing people where to go for relief supplies. We should make it a goal to provide such public service announcements electronically by using personal computer communication. However, the then president of Nippon Telegraph and Telephone Corporation (NTT), Mr. Junichiro Miyazu, admitted that NTT was not entirely certain that a bulletin board system would make a viable business.

We need to overcome such rigid thinking and look for alternative means of communication, including radio and satellite technology, in order to surmount obstacles and save lives in a time of emergency.

KEY POINT

In crisis management, it is essential to make full use of every communication medium available.

Recommendations

Disaster-prone areas must:

1. Build a wireless communication system that can function in an emergency;
2. Build a personal computer communication system that can function in an emergency.

Case **3**

How Government Response is Crucial

It is important for individuals to have their own contingency plans. However, many problems that arise from a major disaster are beyond an individual's capacity to solve them.

Mr. Kazuhiko Arano, who survived the Great Hanshin-Awaji Earthquake, commented on how both the central and local governments were slow in responding to the situation. He said, "Don't expect assistance from the government … the best sources of assistance are large supermarkets, individuals, and then local government, in that order."

As a citizen, I sincerely hope the Japanese government will try harder to do a better job the next time round because what individuals can do at the time of a major disaster is quite limited.

For example, it is almost certain some of the old housing for government workers will be completely destroyed if an earthquake of more than level 6 on the Japanese seismic scale hits the Hanshin-Awaji area. Yet, until the government decides to rebuild them, there is nothing you can do about it as an individual, even if you are a government employee.

If an ordinary citizen were to express a concern about an old government building in the neighborhood that might collapse should a major earthquake occur, they would have much less influence and it is very unlikely that anything will be done immediately.

The same can be said about older bridges, expressways and tunnels. Unless you have an exceptionally strong political influence or a ferocious tenacity in communicating the high risk of their collapse, their reconstruction or repair would usually take years. Of course, if structural concrete blocks were to fall out of a tunnel, then inspections will be conducted immediately.

After the Great Hanshin-Awaji Earthquake and the following volcano eruption, Japan revealed to the world that its **emergency evacuation centers** were less than satisfactory. However, we have yet to see concerted efforts to improve the evacuation centers in quake and other natural disaster-prone areas.

Thus, countermeasures must go beyond individual efforts and include government support, otherwise contingency planning will fail.

KEY POINTS

Most countermeasures against disasters cannot be implemented by the individual.

Even if you feel that you have discovered a countermeasure, you still cannot be successful. No perfect countermeasure exists.

Recommendations

The government should:

1. Improve emergency evacuation centers;
2. Rebuild old, dilapidated housing as much as possible;
3. Reinforce older bridges, expressways and tunnels.

How Supplementary Lifeline Utilities Must Be Developed

Unless we actively take suggestions from specialists on how to develop supplementary lifeline utilities in order to make disaster prevention plans more effective, CP or crisis management will fail.

Generally, **lifeline utilities** mean electricity, gas and water. Professor Kunihiko Hirai of Nagaoka Institute of Design predicts that the current systems, which rely on major electric and gas companies, will be completely disrupted if a disaster of large magnitude occurs. The same thing can be said about water service.

How can we pre-empt such a dire situation? Instead of expending resources to maintain fully functioning systems in times of disaster, he argues for developing supplementary lifeline utilities with the capacity to provide 10 percent of the normal supply.

For example, solar and wind power generators could be utilized as a means of supplementing electricity. For a sewage system, an adequate supply of water should be stored in large tanks to be used for rest rooms in parks and schools in the event of a major disaster. For gas, a supplementary system based on propane should be developed.

The question is how much progress we can make before the next disaster strikes.

In the case of hospitals and medical facilities, an effort should be made to approximate the capacities of the supplementary lifeline utilities at 100 percent.

At all levels of national and local governments, corporations, and individual families, we should place priority on strengthening the supplementary function of lifeline utilities and collaboratively increase their capacities.

KEY POINT

It is essential to develop supplementary lifeline utilities prior to the next disaster.

Recommendations

The government should:

1. Aim to develop supplementary lifeline utilities that can provide 10 percent of normal capacity;
2. Make an effort to increase the capacities of the supplementary lifeline utilities as close to 100 percent as possible at hospitals and other medical facilities.

Case 5

How Voluntary Support Must Be Catered for

In crisis management, it is impossible to respond to every emergent situation as thoroughly as possible. In order to fill this gap, we need to be able not only to take appropriate action but also effectively utilize the help of volunteers.

In the aftermath of a disaster, unforeseen events tend to occur at the same time. It is almost impossible to deal with each one of them thoroughly on a timely basis.

Due to a sudden change of their environment and prolonged anxiety, evacuees who have survived the disaster might develop health problems and need medical attention. In such cases, national or local government assistance may take too long to arrive. This is where **the role of volunteers** becomes important.

At the time of the Great Hanshin-Awaji Earthquake, it was reported that the afflicted area had accepted assistance from 44 nations and regions out of their offers of assistance from 76 nations, regions and organizations, including the United Nations, WHO and EU.

The assistance came in various forms. The United States provided **blankets, drinking water, and cots** through their military forces in Japan. They also sent seismologists, relief supplies, and staff to pitch tents. Switzerland and France provided rescue teams and search dogs. Twenty-four nations, including Mexico, Thailand, South Korea, Australia, China, England, Germany and Russia, provided food, water, clothes, tents and other **relief supplies**. More than 16 nations, including the Netherlands, Italy, Ireland, North Korea, Taiwan and Belgium, provided financial aid.

At the same time, many people from all over Japan were voluntarily participating in rescue activities. For successful crisis management, to be able to receive various forms of assistance and distribute them appropriately on a timely basis is essential.

KEY POINT

Successful crisis management includes the ability to receive and distribute various forms of support from volunteers.

Recommendations

The government should:

1. Build a structure in advance that makes it possible to receive and distribute various forms of support from volunteers;
2. Build and organize a network in advance to facilitate effective volunteer activity in time of crisis.

Case **6**

How to Deal with Psychological Stress

Stress builds up in disaster victims over time. We need to be able to respond to the psychological needs of children, adults and the elderly in a flexible and age-appropriate manner.

In the aftermath of a disaster, many victims are forced to live in highly stressful conditions. For example, earthquake victims have to live in constant fear of strong aftershocks. They would feel helpless after having lost their homes, assets and/or jobs. Furthermore, it is uncertain as to how long they would have to live in a shelter. Over time, stress builds up and takes a toll on their mental and physical health.

It is not possible to eliminate stress entirely, but one can minimize its accumulation. So children should be able to play with other children in the neighborhood. It is very important for them to laugh, exercise, eat and sleep well. It is important for adults to engage in light exercise for recreation, too. They should try to keep a positive outlook and avoid getting too pessimistic.

It should be helpful for them to interact frequently with friends and neighbors who are going through the same experience and find mutual comfort. After the Great Hanshin-Awaji Earthquake, many volunteers engaged victims in **psychologically therapeutic activities** to reduce their stress. In some cases, it is important to consult with a professional.

Elderly people tend to become bedridden. It is important for them to get on their feet and care for themselves as much as possible. They should take up light exercises, if possible. It is not advisable for elderly people with failing energy and stamina to stay in an inconvenient and uncomfortable shelter for longer than necessary. It would be best if accommodation could be prearranged for them in times of disaster. Again, it is important that they participate in psychologically therapeutic activities.

KEY POINT

There are limitations in trying to manage stress on your own.

Recommendations

Disaster victims should:

1. Engage in light exercise for recreation;
2. Interact frequently with friends and neighbors who are going through the same experience and find mutual comfort.

Case 7

Why Ripple Effects Must Be Analysed

Contingencies have dynamic, far-reaching ripple effects which have yet to be fully understood. This makes it difficult to predict what is going to happen subsequently during a natural disaster.

The phrase **"butterfly effect"** refers to the idea that the flap of a butterfly's wings in Tokyo may set off a tornado in Oklahoma. In other words, something seemingly insignificant could grow into monstrous forces of nature that ravage many lives. The term also describes the phenomenon of a tsunami; how the form and force of the waves near the epicenter might be small and ordinary, and yet can grow exponentially more powerful as they approach the shore.

These far-reaching ripple effects of elemental forces are still not fully understood. There must be very complex, non-linear causal relationships among the elements that may cause a chain of events to suddenly develop into a powerful force. Alternatively, small forces may gradually build up massive energy.

Hence, it is important to conduct repeated simulated experiments on an ongoing basis to discover the existence of causal relationships and ascertain their effects from various angles.

For example, in 1961, a meteorologist, Lorenz, was running simulations to re-examine his weather predictions. Before taking a coffee break, he entered the rounded-off data (from six digits to three digits) and left the lab. When he returned from his break, he found totally unexpected and completely different results. This is an example of how natural phenomenon relates to chaos theory, which cannot be explained by simple causal relationships.

No matter how complex and difficult, it is important to deepen our understanding of the dynamic causal relationships and random consequences that might not fit the cause and effect of an event.

KEY POINT

Everything starts out small. (Cicero)

Recommendations

In contingency planning, one must:

1. Investigate the occurrence of unpredictable phenomena through simulations of dynamic events;
2. Continue efforts to improve our ability to predict emergent phenomena by analyzing dynamic causal relationships and far-reaching ripple effects on an ongoing basis.

Case 8

Why Preparation for Disaster Must Include Basic Precautions

CP or crisis management will not succeed as long as there is a deficiency in basic precautions against disaster.

Since late March 1995, Fujitsu Limited has held 16 disaster contingency planning seminars nationwide for their corporate clients, in which they conducted a survey among 2,000 participants on taking precautions against disasters. The results revealed that 55 percent of the responding companies had done nothing to protect their **computer systems against earthquakes** (*Nippon Keizai Shimbun*, **30 August 1995**).

When compared by industry, more than 80 percent of the companies in the insurance and securities sectors were taking some kind of anti-earthquake measures; on the other hand, educational and medical institutions were behind in their efforts.

Almost 30 percent of the companies surveyed were taking some **measures to protect their computer hardware** (e.g., placing them on a quake-absorbing base). Yet only a small percentage of the companies were taking **precautions against data loss** (e.g., backing it up at multiple places). Furthermore, only 44.5 percent of the companies were taking some action to protect their computer system in case of disaster (e.g., having dual communication lines).

In May 1995, the Tokyo Metropolitan Government surveyed 3,000 residents, of which 2,220 responded. It revealed that 52 percent of the respondents had purchased **flashlights, radios, drinking water, and first-aid kits** — of which 24 percent had purchased these disaster supplies after the Great Hanshin-Awaji Earthquake.

At the same time, it was found that approximately 85 percent of the respondents did not know where the nearest water supply facilities from their homes were. Also, 86 percent of the respondents feared the possibility of a major earthquake.

As seen from the above, both businesses and individuals expressed concern about a potential major earthquake, and yet they seemed to be insufficiently prepared for one. It is important to further our efforts to better prepare ourselves against a disaster.

KEY POINT

A survey conducted by the Tokyo Metropolitan Government revealed that 85 percent of the respondents did not know where the nearest water supply facilities were.

Recommendations

To prepare for disaster, one must:

1. Find out the location of water facilities and emergency evacuation center nearest one's home.
2. Find out the location of water facilities and emergency evacuation center nearest one's office.

What to Do in the Event of a Tsunami

A major earthquake can set off not only fires but also tsunamis, depending on the location of its epicenter. Therefore, it is important to be prepared for either case. Regardless, the situation is of great urgency and requires prompt action.

When a major undersea earthquake occurs, a warning about the possibility of tsunami will be issued promptly. However, the warning might not be released immediately after the earthquake. Instead, information on the earthquake itself, such as its magnitude, time and location, will be reported first.

Meanwhile, a tsunami could be forming. Depending on conditions, a giant tsunami could crash ashore within five minutes of an earthquake occurrence. The earthquake that struck at 10:17 PM on 12 July 1993 off the southwestern coast of Hokkaido, Japan's northernmost island, registered 7.8 on the Richter scale. Since this quake was centered under the sea, there was strong concern about the generation of a tsunami. As anticipated, in less than five minutes after the earthquake, a giant tsunami over 20 meters high struck Okushiri Island.

Under such circumstances, we cannot wait for a tsunami advisory on the television. Because the above mentioned earthquake happened late at night and set off fire and landslides simultaneously, many people failed to escape in time. The death toll, including those still missing, reached 230 and the number of homes that were partially or completely destroyed hit 1,009. Some survivors who anticipated a tsunami following the major earthquake, barely made it by racing up a hill as fast as they could in their pyjamas in the dark. When they looked back, they actually saw their homes getting swept away by the roaring waters.

As a **tsunami countermeasure**, it is most important to take prompt action and evacuate as quickly as possible.

KEY POINT

When an earthquake's epicenter is located on the ocean floor, a major tsunami could occur even when the quake intensity is low.

Recommendations

When a tsunami strikes:

1. Everyone must evacuate as quickly as possible when an earthquake's epicenter is located on the ocean floor and in the vicinity of their home;
2. It is most important to move rapidly to higher ground.

How to Distinguish Between Tsunami Advisories: Warning and Watch

In some cases a tsunami warning is issued even when there is no felt earthquake.

A **tsunami warning** or **watch** is issued by the authorities and disseminated by radio, television or vehicles with public address systems, usually within two or three minutes after an earthquake occurs.

A tsunami warning can be categorized into two types: high tsunami and tsunami. The former is an advisory against the possibility of a big tsunami with the water level as high as three meters (with average about 1 m high). The latter is an advisory against one with the water level as high as two meters (with average about 10 cm high).

A tsunami watch can be categorized into four types: tsunami watch, no tsunami, tsunami warning clear, tsunami watch clear. Tsunami watch means "there might be a tsunami with the water level as high as 10 cm." No tsunami means "there is no danger of a tsunami."

However, a tsunami is not always triggered by a major earthquake. There are cases where a tsunami warning is issued when there is no felt earthquake.

In that case, everyone must get away from the beach as quickly as possible and evacuate to a pre-designated area promptly.

Earthquake Disaster Prevention Guide (1995), compiled by the Printing Bureau of the Finance Ministry under the general editorship of the Fire and Disaster Prevention Department of the Home Affairs Ministry, advises that people should move away from the seashore and go to a pre-designated evacuation area as quickly as possible not only after a strong earthquake (above level 4 on the Japanese seismic scale), but also after a relatively small yet prolonged earthquake with slow undulating movements that last for a while.

When there is no pre-designated evacuation area, one must proceed to higher ground.

KEY POINT

A Tsunami can be caused by a relatively small earthquake.

Recommendations

Everyone must:

1. Familiarize themselves with the vocabulary used in the tsunami advisory;
2. Understand the difference between a tsunami warning and watch.

Case 11

The Hospital's Role in Crisis Management

For crisis management and CP to be successful, hospitals must have effective measures to deal with natural disasters.

Professor Shoji Shinozuka of Waseda University had said, "We were far from being well-prepared for a big disaster when the Great Hanshin-Awaji Earthquake hit. First, the governor of the stricken area, who is the highest level government official according to the Basic Law on Natural Disasters, spent as many as three hours inside the government building after the quake. Second, nobody was on duty at the National Land Agency, which is supposed to be in charge of disaster prevention." (*Yomiuri Shimbun*, **17 July 1997**). However, what is more important at the time of disaster is whether hospitals are well-equipped with anti-disaster measures, which will allow them to fulfill their primary function to save human lives.

The injured will be taken to a nearby hospital. Those severely injured, in particular, will require urgent care, but the question is whether the hospital will be sufficiently equipped to attend to them immediately.

In an emergency, a large number of people with life-threatening conditions will be brought to hospital. Yet, in many cases, there are not enough doctors and nurses who can treat them.

Or, at a multi-storied hospital, it will be difficult to move or evacuate patients without the use of elevators. Furthermore, if the electric power goes out, it will be impossible to perform operations without gas-powered electric generators.

At the time of the Great Hanshin-Awaji Earthquake, many hospitals had **emergency power generators**, yet most of them were water-cooled models and could not be used when the water supply was cut off.

The then director of the Nippon Medical School Chiba Hokuso Hospital, Dr. Yasuhiro Yamamoto, urged that hospitals should switch from water-cooled generators to **air-cooled** ones as soon as possible.

It has also been pointed out that although a just-in-time inventory system of medicine is effective in stock and disposal cost reduction, it is seriously flawed in that it will not have enough reserves in the event of emergency.

KEY POINT

One of the most important missions of hospitals is to save human lives at the time of disaster.

Recommendations

All hospitals:

1. Should be equipped with air-cooled electric generators;
2. Should have stockpiles of medicine available for emergencies.

Why Hospitals Must Have Continual Access to Water

At the time of the Great Hanshin-Awaji Earthquake, some hospitals were unable to perform operations on patients requiring urgent care because their water tanks were damaged. In order to provide effective medical treatment in emergencies, hospitals must have quake-resistant water storage tanks.

It is most important to **maintain lifeline utilities at hospitals** in emergencies. However, in a major earthquake, hospitals could lose their supply of electricity, gas, and water.

In the case of the Great Hanshin-Awaji Earthquake, some hospitals lost access to water, which is indispensable for hospital operations, because their water storage tanks were damaged. Consequently, they were unable to provide patients with certain kinds of treatment such as dialysis.

Based on this experience, the highest priority should be given to the installation of power generators and quake-resistant water storage tanks at hospitals as disaster countermeasures.

If it is difficult for a hospital to secure sufficient amounts of water in case of a disaster, they might consider pre-arranging to obtain water from a nearby swimming pool with a water purification system.

However, if the swimming pool is meant to supply several days' worth of drinking water to disaster victims in the area, then it is not advisable to use it unless absolutely necessary. In that case, it might be a good idea to consider having water shipped in by air as part of an alternative emergency plan.

The decision to transport patients by air to a hospital outside the disaster area for treatment, or to have water shipped to a designated hospital in the disaster area, needs to be made promptly and on a case-by-case basis. Some factors to be considered include the capacity of the hospital, the degree of damage incurred to the facility, and the number of patients requiring urgent care.

At the time of the Great Hanshin-Awaji Earthquake, at least several hundreds of patients reportedly required urgent treatment.

KEY POINT

Hospitals need continual access to water for patient treatment and care.

Recommendations

Hospitals must:

1. Equip themselves with quake-resistant water tanks as well as power generators;
2. Consider having water shipped in by air in an emergency.

How Schools Can Be Used as Evacuation Centers (1)

Use school facilities as an evacuation center to make contingency planning more effective.

At the time of the Great Hanshin-Awaji Earthquake, **school facilities** were not necessarily designated as evacuation sites. Yet they turned out to be invaluable shelters for local residents.

It is important to consider how we can make the school facilities, which are not necessarily suitable as a shelter, more disaster-resistant and functional as an emergency evacuation center.

In 1996, the Ministry of Education (currently the Ministry of Education, Culture, Sports, Science and Technology) announced their decision to strengthen the disaster-prevention function of public schools (*Nippon Keizai Shimbun*, **23 August 1995**). Of course, this effort should be extended to national and private schools as well. To push ahead with this initiative, we need to first identify what are the minimum requirements to be met if a school were to be used as an emergency evacuation center. Then models of such schools could be adopted throughout the country.

As school facilities mostly come under the jurisdiction of the Ministry of Education (currently the Ministry of Education, Culture, Sports, Science and Technology), the Ministry needs to work in coordination with other ministries and agencies to make the earth-quake disaster prevention schemes more reliable and effective. These ministries and agencies include the Ministry of Home Affairs (cur-rently the Ministry of Internal Affairs and Communications), the Ministry of Construction (currently the Ministry of Land, Infrastructure and Transportation), the Fire and Disaster Management Agency, and the Meteorological Agency.

We need to draw up different scenarios depending on when a disaster occurs. For example, the extent or degree of disaster-control functions that schools are expected to perform should vary, depend-ing on if a disaster happens when teachers, staff members and students are in school, or on their way to school, or when nobody is in school.

Further, we need to take other factors into consideration in decid-ing on the minimum requirements to be met by the school, such as whether there are other disaster-prevention facilities in the neighbor-hood. We need to have flexible plans for different conditions to make disaster-prevention schemes more effective.

KEY POINT

Schools make appropriate evacuation centers if they meet certain requirements

Recommendations

All schools should:

1. Strengthen their potential disaster-prevention function to prepare for their use as an emergency evacuation center;
2. Meet minimum requirements for their use as emergency evacua-tion centers — and this should be modelled throughout the country as soon as possible.

How Schools Can Be Used as Evacuation Centers (2)

It is important to consider the duration and number of people that schools, used as evacuation shelters, can accommodate in the worst-case scenario.

When planning to use school facilities as an **emergency evacuation shelter**, it is important to think first about the duration and number of people that a particular school will be able to accommodate. Merely specifying the maximum duration will not be helpful because difficulties will arise when the number of disaster victims significantly exceeds the optimum capacity.

It is probably reasonable to set three days as a minimum base number. However, unless we have a good grasp of the facility's capacity limitation, it is not useful to discuss its minimum requirements.

Instead of setting an arbitrary number as the absolute upper limit, it is more important to take into account the area's population and other potential evacuation facilities and then form an estimate of how many people will need to be accommodated in this particular facility in the worst case scenario. This is important because there is a possibility that disaster prevention planning could turn out to be ineffective at a critical moment.

Minimally, what will be needed in a school are accommodations for people to sleep, to store potable water and food (temporarily stored in an unoccupied classroom), and to prepare meals using emergency fuel (e.g., propane gas), and a **swimming pool** for water storage. Further, a purification system will be needed to convert swimming pool water to drinking water during the emergency.

According to estimates by the Ministry of Education (currently the Ministry of Education, Culture, Sports, Science and Technology), an eight-lane, 25-meter-long swimming pool has the capacity of storing about 400 tons of water, which is enough to serve about 800 people for three days (*Nippon Keizai Shimbun,* **23 August 1995**). Additional considerations **include reinforcing classrooms against earthquakes** and establishing **stress management programs for the disaster victims**.

KEY POINT

There must be accurate estimates of the housing capacity of school facilities as an emergency shelter to address any shortages in advance.

Recommendations

Schools should have:

1. Facilities that can be used to store water and food in an emergency;
2. Facilities for cooking and serving meals;
3. A purification system installed.

How to Get the Injured to Hospital

When an earthquake with a magnitude of 7, or a Japanese seismic intensity of 5, occurs, it is crucial that the emergency medical service is ready to dispatch ambulances promptly upon request.

It is unlikely that an earthquake of this magnitude will cause extensive damage to emergency medical facilities. In most cases, emergency medical services should be able to dispatch **ambulances** upon request.

It is highly desirable for ambulances to be equipped with a geographical information system (GIS), with which they can see not only the condition of the roads but also the location of obstructions along the route. Without the GIS, it could take much longer for an ambulance to get to its destination. In the worst case, they might not be able to get to the destination at all.

The Off Miyagi prefecture earthquake of 1978, which struck around 5:14 p.m., registered 7.4 on the Richter scale and 5 on the Japanese seismic intensity scale. Although as many as 6,757 houses were partially or completely destroyed, deaths were confined to 28. Yet, emergency phone lines were flooded with calls for ambulances and the response rate was reportedly less than 10 percent. (Ambulances managed to serve only 28 out of 9,300 injured persons.)

Furthermore, the power failure caused by the earthquake paralyzed the communication networks. The ambulances on the road lost radio contact with the dispatcher at the emergency radio base. To make matters worse, traffic lights did not function due to the loss of power, which caused havoc to the transportation system in the area.

Under such chaotic circumstances, local residents need to take some emergency measures themselves. It is very important for them to obtain knowledge and skills through disaster-prevention training.

KEY POINT

During disasters, emergency medical services will be inundated with requests for ambulances.

Recommendations

If a disaster strikes your area:

1. Use other means of transportation (e.g., car, motorbike) to take an injured person to a hospital as soon as possible, when an ambulance is not available;
2. Seek help from a neighborhood disaster-prevention and rescue organization when it is not feasible to transport an injured person yourself.

How to Call an Ambulance

At a time of disaster, we may encounter a situation where we need to call an ambulance for an injured person. In a situation like this where every minute counts, it is important to follow the emergency call procedures and explain the situation and your location clearly and concisely.

In the aftermath of a major earthquake, emergency phone lines will be flooded with calls reporting numerous injuries.

In order to enable the highest number of calls to be connected, calls must be kept short. However, we tend to take up a lot more time than necessary in an emergency because we are agitated. To avoid this, we should have a basic understanding of **how to call an ambulance**.

After dialing 1-1-9 (to call an ambulance), follow the next four steps to be concise.

First, say, "This is an emergency." Second, tell them your name, address, and a nearby **prominent landmark** (e.g., a building or sign) or two to help the emergency crew locate you. Third, tell them what has happened and what the current condition of the injured person is. In other words, clearly explain the **urgency of the situation**. And fourth, which often gets forgotten, tell them **someone will be signaling in front**

of the house. That can significantly help to shorten the time needed to locate you.

We can expedite the arrival of an ambulance by following the above steps. It might be a good idea to have the procedures recorded on a piece of paper near the phone.

KEY POINT

When calling for an ambulance, it is critical to explain the urgency of the situation and give accurate and precise directions.

Recommendations

When calling for an ambulance, you should:

1. After dialing 1-1-9, say, "This is an emergency;"
2. Decide before on a recognizable landmark nearby to guide the driver to your home;
3. Have somebody stand in front of your house after making the call.

How to Deal with Rumors

Regardless of whether it is induced by a natural or man-made disaster, false rumors tend to develop from the chaos. Crisis management will not succeed if people blindly believe rumors without ascertaining their authenticity.

In a time of disaster, whether it is an earthquake or terrorist attack, communication systems get shut down and **misleading rumors** tend to arise from the chaos.

"There was a bigger earthquake in such and such area", "A huge tsunami is coming tonight", "Our drinking water has become contaminated". In most cases, this kind of information gets distorted in the process of circulation due to fear and spreads rapidly, setting off a chain reaction.

In an emergency, it is prudent not to blindly believe hearsay. We should always try to verify its authenticity with a reliable source, such as the local government and mass media.

At the time of the Great Kanto Earthquake of 1923, many people were seized with intense fear and panic due to insufficient fire control service, malfunctioning fire hydrants, collapsed bridges, and disrupted communication systems. It was further exacerbated by a rumor that petroleum tanks had exploded and everyone was going to die.

In order to deal with such rumors effectively, it is important to stay calm and take the minimum steps required to **check safety conditions** after an earthquake has stopped, without worrying too much about the possibility of aftershocks. These include turning off a stove, shutting off the gas, moving flammable substances to a safe location, and reinforcing the home.

Then, tune in to a public or private broadcast on the radio or television to verify the authenticity of the information related to the earthquake, tsunami, subsequent damage, and rescue efforts. In addition, try to sift through the information by using a cell-phone and **PC communication**, if possible.

KEY POINT

At a time of disaster, it is important to stay calm and collected so that you can have good judgment.

Recommendations

In an emergency, one should:

1. Verify hearsay with a public or private broadcaster;
2. Verify hearsay by using the Internet.

Case 18

How to Prepare for the Breakdown of Electrical Substations (Lifeline Utilities): An Example from the Taiwan Earthquake

If electrical substations break down, even when buildings sustain little damage, it can have a serious impact on political, economic and civil activities.

The Taiwan Earthquake, which occurred at 1:47 a.m. (local time) on September 21, 1999, originated in the middle of Taiwan, but caused a massive blackout in the northern part of the country, including Taipei. It took as many as 18 days before electricity was fully restored on October 8.

One of the main causes for the massive blackout was the breakdown of two major substations near Taipei: the Tienlun and Chungliao ultra-high voltage substations. Although 60 percent of the country's demand for power was concentrated in the north, many of the main power plants were located in the south. When transmission lines from the south to the north broke down, the system's capacity to supply power plummeted drastically and caused the massive blackout in the north. It can be said that this earthquake hit "Taiwan's Achilles' heel".

Fortunately, Taiwan Power Company had taken a lesson from the Great Hanshin Earthquake and compiled an anti-earthquake measure manual. According to the manual, the restoration priorities were given to government agencies, hospitals, and transportation and communication systems. Among the various government agencies, the Hsinchu Science Park Administration, an internationally influential high-tech industry park, was given the highest priority with power restored on September 24, only three days after the quake (*Nikkei Industry News*, **9 December 1999**).

However, most people in the area were left without power for days and had to drive on roads without operable traffic lights. To maintain fairness among the regions, power was rationed to residents according to geography and different availability time-slots were allotted, such as from 7 a.m. to 3 p.m. in region A and 3 p.m. to 11 p.m. in region B.

Yet, despite attempts at fairness, certain regions were given priority over others. People in areas where the recovery of power was delayed voiced much dissatisfaction. To pre-empt similar disruptions, it is essential for each business and organization to voluntarily install a backup power system to **maintain the function of lifeline utilities** in an emergency.

KEY POINT

Consider the relative importance of lifeline utilities on a routine basis during ordinary times.

Recommendations

Businesses and organizations in earthquake-prone areas must:

1. Install an emergency power generator;
2. Familiarize themselves with the emergency measures in case a substation breaks down and prepare for an emergency.

How a Disaster Can Be Turned Into a Lesson

The Sumatra Earthquake Tsunami of 2004 caused the worst damage in recorded history. This is partly attributed to the lack of knowledge about the danger of tsunamis on the part of the residents and tourists in the affected areas.

A huge earthquake with a magnitude of 9 occurred around 8 a.m. (local time) on 26 December 2004, approximately 160 km off the west coast of Sumatra, Indonesia, at a depth of 10 km below sea level. This earthquake caused devastating damage to more than 10 countries with coasts bordering the Indian Ocean. The poorest segments of the populations and tourists were the hardest hit. It was reported that giant tsunamis that followed the quake inundated the coastal areas with waves 10 meter-high on average (but as high as 34 meters in some places) at speed of 700 kilometers per hour. It was one of the deadliest natural disasters in history, which killed or left missing more than 300,000.

It has been pointed out that it was not the earthquake itself, but the resulting massive tsunamis which crashed ashore at tremendous speeds that caused so much death and destruction in this disaster. The fact that most of the hard-hit areas were beach resorts, such as Thailand's Phuket area, contributed to the high death toll. Many tourists were spending their Christmas holidays at the resorts. They were reportedly from Sweden, Germany, England, France and other European countries.

It is important to note that these resorts had not been hit by tsunamis before and neither had the tourists. The Thailand Meteorological Agency did not issue a tsunami warning or watch after the earthquake. Nor did they issue an emergency evacuation advisory in the coastal area.

Local people reportedly went out to the beach after the tide receded, drawn by the curious sight. Many of the tourist victims from Europe lived far from the ocean and probably had little knowledge of the danger of tsunamis. The damage of this unfortunate natural disaster was exacerbated by both human negligence and ignorance.

Devastating disasters which should have been recounted from generation to generation have not been ingrained in people's memories. Many years ago in Japan, a book by the title of *The Straw Torch*, had talked about the ravaging power of a tsunami and the importance of prompt evacuation. This story was introduced to the United States and Great Britain at the end of the 19th century in a chapter titled "A Living God", in the book **Gleanings in Buddha-Fields**.

A tsunami had crashed ashore in Wakayama Prefecture 32 hours after the 8.4-magnitude Tokai earthquake in 1854. An old man who had anticipated it lit a torch made of rice straw and led villagers to high ground, thus saving many lives.

This story was used as a Japanese reader in elementary schools for 10 years from 1937. Many local governments still use it to teach disaster prevention in elementary schools. This is a theme that is recognized as important in the elementary school curriculum. Learning the devastating power of a tsunami at a relatively young age is an effective way to raise public awareness and should be continued.

KEY POINT

Succeeding generations need to learn from historical disasters, so that they do not repeat the same mistakes.

Recommendations

Schools should:

1. Use audio-visual materials to teach about disaster experiences at home and overseas;
2. Incorporate lessons learned from disasters in the elementary school curriculum.

The Mid-Niigata Prefecture Earthquake (1): How the Media was Unhelpful

Mass media should refrain from repeating images and information that stir up fear in the audience.

According to a survey conducted by the Niigata Prefecture Hotel and Inn Association in November 2004, the number of cancellations of reservations for overnight stays and banquets between 23 October the day of the earthquake, and 10 November reached 312,000 and continued to rise afterward. The average cancellation rate within the prefecture was about 80 percent, but there were some areas where the cancellation rate was more than 90 percent. The total economic loss was estimated at eight billion yen.

Although the area along the Niigata and Nagano Prefectures border sustained little damage, the number of skiers in Echigo-Yuzawa up until 5 January was down by 30 percent from the previous year because the earthquake struck just before the ski season started. There was a rash of cancellations of reservations for banquets and weddings in the disaster-stricken area as well.

The main industry in this quake-stricken area is tourism. Winter, particularly, is the most profitable season. Some people might have acted out of consideration for the victims and refrained from engaging in festivities in the disaster area. Still, many cancelled their reservations out of fear that the area might not be safe. Thus, it can be said that tourism in the disaster-stricken area suffered **damage from harmful rumors**.

Damage from harmful rumors means "economic loss attributed to ungrounded, unsubstantiated information". A person (or persons) who starts such a rumor passes along information as if it were a fact without confirming its authenticity.

Mass media, particularly television and radio, send correspondents to a disaster site to report on the extent of the damage, and the scale and character of the earthquake. They also feature experts and analysts who talk about lessons to be learned from the disaster. The audience, constantly bombarded by information, develops an ominous impression as well as fear.

The TV media particularly, tends to focus on presenting negative information and rarely does follow-up reports after normal operations are restored. As a result, the audience believes that the stricken area is still unsafe. A spokesperson for the Niigata Prefecture Hotel and Inn Association expressed regret over the financial distress caused by the mass media. He said, "The excessive media coverage was the biggest factor that caused so much economic damage to the business in the area. We asked the media to report then the areas adjacent to the central region of Niigata Prefecture were safe, but they were slow to respond."

Instead of focusing on sensational images or information, mass media should report the story objectively, responsibly and thoroughly until the resumption of normal operations. The mission of public broadcasting is to cover the disaster until safety and order are restored.

KEY POINT

When only provided with unsettling information, the audience tends to overreact out of fear. The media should take the responsibility of covering a disaster story until all concerns for safety have been objectively met.

Recommendations

1. The media should report facts objectively and impartially, instead of focusing on certain information to attract audience attention.
2. When it becomes clear that damage has been done by misinformation, the local government, industry and trade groups or businesses concerned should set the record straight.

Case 21

The Mid-Niigata Prefecture Earthquake (2): How to Keep Means of Communication Open

In the aftermath of a major earthquake, ordinary telecommunication lines tend to get severed or flooded by heavy access. Ensuring communication connection in an emergency is one of the most important tasks.

The backbone communication networks of Nippon Telegraph and Telephone East Corporation (NTT East) sustained serious damage by landslides triggered by the earthquake. Many of the main communication lines got severed in the area along the Shinano River, particularly around Nagaoka City, where IP telephone lines converged. As a result, a total of 4,450 subscribed telephone services were disrupted in the towns of Oguni and Koshiji and the village of Yamakoshi.

After a large earthquake, many people outside the stricken area are concerned about the safety of those affected by the disaster and flood telephone lines by trying to call them. Except for emergency phone lines, NTT and mobile phone companies place restrictions on access to regular phone lines before they get saturated. In fact, after the Mid-Niigata Prefecture Earthquake, restrictions were placed on the transmission of voice data over NTT subscribed phones and cell phones in the disaster area.

Nonetheless, people were able to use IP phones, send and receive e-mail from mobile phones, and access the Internet in areas where communication lines were available. An IP phone is a telephone service which uses the Internet connection to convert voice data to packets. To avoid the disruption of e-mail usage and web access as much as possible in the aftermath of the disaster, NTT DoCoMo placed different levels of restrictions on the voice service and i-mode service (which allows customers to connect to the Internet and gives them instant access to various sites using their cell phones).

Yet, this kind of communication system will be disrupted if the batteries which power the routers and servers run out, the networks themselves get severed, or the communication base station is damaged.

KEY POINT

Data packet transmission service may be available at the time of a disaster, but necessary subsystems (networks, batteries, etc.) need to function as well.

Recommendations

1. In a time of disaster, mobile phone companies should place restrictions on access to networks based on the type of data transmission method and continue to provide data packet transmission service.
2. Residents should have an extra supply of batteries and backup electric power generator.

The Mid-Niigata Prefecture Earthquake (3): Why it is Critical to Restore a Region's Industry

---

Ensuring safety in the disaster area is a top priority. Yet, the reconstruction of the area requires more than merely restoring the stability of daily life.

Manufacturing is a main industry in the central Niigata region. There are large-scale automotive part manufacturing operations in Nagaoka City and electro-mechanical component manufacturing plants in Ojiya City. If manufacturing operations cannot be restored quickly, the economic output in the area is estimated to go down by 200 billion yen a year and 13,000 jobs will be lost.

Yet, the mid-Niigata region has traditionally been known for agriculture. It is a prominent grain belt, famous for its high-quality rice, for example, the Koshi-hikari brand, from the Uonuma area. The brewing of alcoholic beverages and manufacturing of snack foods made from rice is also popular in the region. There are quite a few communities where agriculture is the key industry. The primary agricultural industry employed over 10 percent of the workers in 15 cities, towns and villages in the region. According to Niigata Prefecture, the agriculture, forestry and fishery-related economic losses caused by the earthquake amounted to 1.3 billion yen as of November 2004. Also, serious damage was done to businesses engaged in raising nishiki-goi, an exotic decorative variety of koi fish, in the villages of Ojiya and Yamakoshi.

A stable housing environment and close proximity to the crop-growing fields are the minimum requirements for the success of agriculture. There is now growing concern that this earthquake may have caused many farmers to **give up their agricultural operations**. Continuous farmland preservation helps the conservation of the natural environment in the area. If many people abandon farming and leave the land, it will have significant ramifications for environmental conservation and thus, a far-reaching effect beyond the mere decline of an industry.

The government gives the highest priority to helping disaster victims put their lives back in order by ensuring their **security, food**, and **housing**. They take a step-by-step approach to reconstruct the disaster-stricken area to a minimal level, by following the National Disaster Act and National Disaster Victims Relief Law.

However, in a mountainous area interspersed with fields, such as the central Niigata region, ensuring housing by building temporary living facilities is far from enough for the reconstruction of the community. Without assistance for the **restoration of their traditional industry**, many of the disaster victims will not be able to make a living, let alone reconstruct the community as a whole.

KEY POINT

The reconstruction of a disaster-stricken area should be handled on the basis of medium- and long-term needs that take the restoration of the regional specific industry into consideration.

Recommendations

In reconstructing a disaster area, the government should:

1. Take the regional, geographical and industrial characteristics of the area into account and grant exceptions to the Natural Disaster Victims Relief-related bills as appropriate;
2. Make it the highest priority to help the disaster victims put their lives back in order.

The Mid-Niigata Prefecture Earthquake (4): Why there should be Private Insurance against Earthquake Damage

In recent years, large-scale natural disasters have been happening more frequently. This has led to the improvement of legal support for disaster victims. Yet, a comprehensive support system to aid the fundamental recovery of victims' lives is still under development.

Earthquake damage in the Mid-Niigata Prefecture was exacerbated by **heavy snowfalls** that occurred shortly thereafter. **Figuring out how to apply laws related to disaster relief** remains an issue.

Mr. Kamimura, a lecturer at Nagaoka University of Technology, said, "Nineteen lives were lost in the accidents during snow removal operations. It's actually 20 if you include the accident in Yamakoshi Village in which a snow-plow truck driver fell into the river while working." He pointed out that despite a high number of deaths and casualties from heavy snowfall and subsequent removal operations, damage from snow is not treated as a disaster.

Many houses in the central Niigata region collapsed under the weight of heavy snow that fell shortly after the earthquake. While an evacuation order was in effect, the quake victims were not allowed to return home. Thus, they stayed in a shelter while worrying about the condition of their housing. They would have wanted to return home to remove the snow from the roof of their house before the onset of winter to avoid the collapse of their home.

The Natural Disaster Victims Relief Law addresses the improvement of a disaster victim's housing environment. Yet, this law is limited to assistance for the demolition-related expense of a house damaged by a disaster and does not cover reconstruction or repairs of the house. Since a house is considered a personal asset, the government limits the use of public funds for this purpose.

It is prudent for the property owner to protect their personal assets with **insurance against earthquake damage**. However, private earthquake insurance usually only covers the damage to personal properties incurred by fire, destruction, and loss directly caused by an earthquake, volcanic eruption, or tsunami. Earthquake insurance might not cover damage caused by a combination of an earthquake and heavy snow.

KEY POINT

The government will not insure against the loss of personal assets incurred by a natural disaster.

Recommendations

Homeowners should:

1. Protect their own personal assets;
2. Purchase private earthquake insurance, just in case.

How to Plan for Evacuation During Torrential Rain

It is difficult to predict exactly when torrential rain is going to occur, how long it is going to last, and how severe it is going to become. It could suddenly bring about substantial damage.

A record **torrential rain storm** occurred in a localized area of the central Niigata Prefecture (Nagaoka and Sanjo districts) and Fukushima Prefecture (Aizu region) in July 2004. It caused the banks of five tributaries in the Shinano River system to burst at 11 points which concurrently created landslides. The disaster caused many casualties, including 16 deaths, as well as tremendous housing damage.

Over time, **torrential rain** becomes increasingly dangerous and can cause substantial damage to residents in the area. A mudslide caused by a torrential rain is a typical example. In the mountain areas, a mudslide tends to occur on the hillside when the amount of rain exceeds the water retention limit of the soil. Similarly, flooding occurs when the amount of rainfall exceeds the capacity of a river. Either way, damage can be immense.

To avoid serious damage, it is important to tune into the weather news bulletin once the downpour starts and act on the latest information before the situation escalates. According to a survey by the Hiroi Research Team at the University of Tokyo (*Residents' Behaviors and the*

Circulation of Disaster Information at the Time of the Torrential Rain in Niigata and Fukushima in 2004), almost everybody (97.7 percent) in the affected area wanted "authorities to issue **an evacuation order and instructions** at the earliest practical stage, even if there is a chance that it might not turn out as severely as predicted."

If local authorities and mass media, especially television and radio, start providing information on the torrential rain and the extent of damage at an early point, residents can avoid missing an opportunity to evacuate voluntarily even before the official evacuation order is issued. Access to accurate and timely weather information will help residents correctly assess the situation and make rational judgments.

Authorities should evaluate the extent of damage promptly and work with the media to provide evacuation information sooner rather than later to protect the safety of the residents.

KEY POINT

Torrential rain can cause substantial damage. It is critical to start gathering information at an early stage to minimize damage. Local authorities should work with the media and prepare to provide an evacuation order and instructions as soon as possible.

Recommendations

1. The authorities should carefully evaluate the optimum timing of when to issue an evacuation order and instructions to the residents sooner rather than later;

2. They should prepare the wireless simultaneous public address system to make the speedy transmission of information possible in a disaster-stricken area.

3. People who have never experienced a serious natural disaster before tend to under-estimate the severity of the situation. Everyone must try to start gathering accurate information at an early stage of disaster development so that good judgments can be made as to when, how and where to evacuate.

Case **25**

How to Prepare for Hazardous Secondary Effects

**Research on large-scale earthquake prediction and potential dam-
age is progressing. It aims at estimating direct damage caused by an
earthquake in inland areas. With a large earthquake, however, the
potential danger from petrochemical industrial complexes in coastal
areas needs to be considered as well.**

The Central Disaster Prevention Council is spearheading research on
damage prediction and disaster prevention against potential large-
scale earthquakes in Japan (e.g., a Southern Kanto earthquake, a Tokai
earthquake, an Eastern Nankai earthquake, a Nankai earthquake).

Anticipated damage by a large earthquake includes collapsing
houses, structures and earth, catastrophic fires in urban and residential areas, and the subsidence of structures caused by the liquefaction
of the ground. In addition, damage from a tsunami should be
considered in coastal areas.

We need to further consider secondary damage as well. For
example, **petrochemical industrial complexes in coastal areas have
a high risk of catching fire** as a result of a massive earthquake.

Many of the areas where large earthquakes are predicted have
attracted capital investments for heavy chemicals industry operations.
This occurred during the high-growth period of the Japanese economy

from the 1960s to the beginning of the 1970s. A seismologist, who used computer simulation of the motions of the petroleum tanks in the Tokyo Bay area, has predicted that more than 60 would burst into flames if a Tokai or Nankai earthquake occurs.

A petroleum tank fire is caused by what is called the "sloshing phenomenon". The tank is vigorously shaken by the earthquake in a direction which coincides with the seismic center. As a result, the oil spills out of the tank and is ignited by sparks from the collision between the floating roof and the side wall. The fire of a naphtha storage tank in Tomakomai City, after the Tokachi offshore earthquake in September 2003, happened as a result of this process.

If the oil leaks through cracks in the tanks into sea water, the situation will be even more dire. It would be extremely difficult to contain or extinguish.

Another concern is **how earthquake-resistant** outdoor petroleum tanks are. Presently there are 1,329 tanks in Japan larger than 550 kiloliter that contain combustible fuel. About 64 percent of these tanks were built before seismic design standards became strengthened, have not had their seismic capacity evaluated, or are yet to be reinforced.

The existing Fire Protection Law requires all tanks to satisfy seismic design standards by 2020. The Fire Defense Agency is working to move up the deadline. Since a large-scale earthquake is a natural disaster that could strike any time, the moving up of the deadline should be done as soon as possible.

The problem is partly due to a lack of urgency on the part of the regulatory authorities toward large-scale production facilities, such as petrochemical complexes. Yet, it is also due to the inability of some production sites to respond quickly to the seismic design and disaster prevention code and standard.

When the fire of a naphtha storage tank in Tomakomai city after the Tokachi offshore earthquake occurred on 26 September 2003, Yokkaichi City which operates many similar production facilities responded very quickly. Several days after the earthquake, the city sent a team of people from the Disaster Prevention Division and the

Safety and Fire Prevention Division to the disaster site. This shows their dedicated efforts to try to learn from the incident about what fire-fighting problems had been experienced and what could have been done to minimize the damage. Then, they announced that they would examine the condition of the local petrochemical tanks in their own city and call an emergency meeting for the local petro-chemical industrial complex establishments.

One of the authors grew up in Suzuka City, adjacent to Yokkaichi. I still remember the strong, offensive odors that we experienced when-ever I rode along Route 23 with my father when I was young. But now the odors are hardly noticeable, thanks to the regulatory author-ities who served as the driving force for the environmental cleanup. Also, state and local governments have worked hard to actively tighten up the regulations. Success came from joint efforts by the rel-evant production facilities and state and local governments. We hope to see more of these pro-active approaches to crisis management against the large-scale earthquakes that have been predicted.

In seismic disaster, it is not enough to consider direct damage; it is imperative that we pay attention to energy facilities, particularly petrochemical complexes. Relevant local governments and regula-tory authorities need to **work hand in hand to improve the safety** of these facilities.

KEY POINT

In the context of earthquake disasters, one must identify and study in advance the potentially most hazardous secondary effects.

Recommendations

The government must:

1. Move up the deadline for satisfying the earthquake-resistance standards for petrochemical complex facilities.
2. Take corrective measures toward the facilities which have yet to meet the earthquake-resistance standards.

3. Consider revising the current Fire Protection Law and ease the regulations regarding firefighting equipment. (It has been pointed out that the inspection and certification system of firefighting equipment specified in the current Fire Protection Law makes it difficult to adopt newly developed, more superior firefighting equipment.)

4. Work with local government to implement some policies to facilitate the last two recommendations of the above three.

Case **26**

What We Can Learn from Hurricane Katrina

In crisis management, a balance of foresight and resource allocation is critical.

Hurricane Katrina was one of the worst natural disasters in U.S. history, which caused a horrifying number of deaths and injuries as well as massive destruction of homes. It also left many ironies and hard lessons.

The first irony is in its name. The Monastery of St. Katrina (Catherine) is a designated World Heritage site located near Mount Sinai, the place where God gave Moses the Ten Commandments. Why did a hurricane named Katrina, which is a symbol of benevolence, end up bringing such devastation to humans?

The second irony is that following the 11 September 2001 terrorist attacks, the **Department of Homeland Security** (**DHS**) was created to develop counter-measures. Subsequently, the **Federal Emergency Management Agency** (**FEMA**) was downgraded from a cabinet level agency and absorbed into DHS. FEMA demonstrated their effectiveness under the Clinton Administration (e.g., a speedy response to an earthquake in Los Angeles and an early evacuation effort at the time of a hurricane in the southeast). Yet, it was intensely criticized for its ineffective, uncoordinated response to Hurricane Katrina, which led its director, Michael Brown, to resign.

The third irony is that the National Guard troops, who were intended to provide evacuation assistance and relief operations, were seriously short staffed to handle disasters of this magnitude. At the time, 40 percent of Mississippi's and 35 percent of Louisiana's National guards were deployed to Iraq. Further, necessary equipment for this kind of disaster — such as Humvees and other vehicles designed to operate in high water conditions, fuel and water tankers, and generators — were not readily available for use.

The fourth irony is that **global warming** might have contributed to this catastrophe. Sir David King, the UK Government's Chief Scientific Adviser said, "It has been known since 1978 that hurricane strength is highly correlated with sea surface temperature. The sea temperature in the Northern Hemisphere has increased by 0.5°C for the past 15 and 20 years. It is easy to conclude that the increased intensity of hurricanes can be correlated to global warming." His comment can be taken as a criticism of the United States for their lack of support for the **Kyoto Protocol**.

And the fifth irony is that the main victims of this hurricane were the poorest 100 thousand population, which accounted for 20 percent of the residents of New Orleans, who did not have means to evacuate themselves. In other words, they did not have cars or credit cards and were unable to find any way out of the city, which led to hundreds of deaths.

KEY POINT

The ability to develop foresight and include unanticipated situations in a disaster prevention and response strategy is critical.

Recommendations

The authorities should:

1. Provide emergency unemployment benefits to people who have lost jobs due to the disaster.

2. Provide long-term emergency shelters to those who have lost their homes due to the disaster.
3. Immediately release stockpiles of food and clothing from government-stocked warehouses throughout the country.
4. Provide food, water, clothes, medicine and other necessities through various business organizations, supermarket chains and drugstores.
5. Deploy large-scale medical teams to the disaster site for epidemic disease prevention.
6. Provide relief through early payment of property damage insurance to victims.
7. Coordinate with national, state and local governments to work together to develop a disaster recovery plan for rapid implementation when needed.
8. Develop a disaster protection and evacuation plan and implement it before the next hurricane and earthquake strikes.

Case **27**

The Great Sichuan Earthquake: Why Wide-Area-Coverage Evacuation Centers are Needed

When a large-scale earthquake disaster strikes, large, sturdy school buildings (or public facilities) serve to forestall the expansion of secondary damage.

On 12 May 2008, a major earthquake of the direct-hit type occurred in the Province of Sichuan, which is located in the central-western part of the People's Republic of China. The catastrophic event came to be known later as the Great Sichuan Earthquake. By "magnitude," a denotation of the scale of seismic severity, the tremor was confirmed to have been of the order of 7.9 to 8.0, counting as one of the severest events of its kind ever to hit any part of the world. According to an announcement dated 4 September 2008 released by a national committee of experts of the Chinese government, the direct damage suffered would amount to a good 845.1 billion yuan (about US$122.4 billion). The same source further states that Sichuan Province accounted for 91.3 percent of the entire earthquake-incurred damage, or 771.6 billion yuan in monetary terms. Since the budgeted general revenue for 2007 was 85.034 billion yuan, a figure released by the financial administration source of the same province, the amount of the earthquake-incurred damage would have corresponded to approximately nine years' worth of the same province's financial revenue, according to some observers.

The Ministry of Civil Affairs of China announced in its 22 July 2008 report that, as of noon, 21 July 2008 local time, the number of those who perished in the disaster was 69,197, and that the injured numbered 374,176, and those missing, 18,222. It is surmised that, as of the time of writing in December 2008, the numbers of dead, wounded and missing persons would have substantially increased.

What has been pointed out as problematic in connection with this catastrophic event is that there was no support system in place for disaster prevention or disaster mitigation applicable at the national level, and that earthquake-resistant building design was not yet widely practiced. It is thought that the slow response in immediate post-tremor life saving and relief operations was at least in part responsible for the spread of the damage. In dealing with circumstances such as this, it becomes a matter of burning urgency to accept offers of assistance from other countries equipped with experience and technology in rescue and relief operations. The Chinese authorities were late in making a political decision to accept such offers, and it may be said that it was this delay in decision-making that resulted in the soaring number of victims.

Reportedly, the number of collapsed and destroyed residential structures is simply staggering. Almost 7,000 school buildings are said to have collapsed in Sichuan Province alone, and more than 10 percent of all victims are believed to have been accounted for by teachers and students crushed to death under collapsing school buildings. The fact that buildings duly complying with earthquake resistance standards were few, alongside the fact that much construction suffered from "corner-cutting" at the hands of builders, certainly contributed to the astounding magnitude of the disaster.

The collapse of great numbers of school buildings in the Great Sichuan Earthquake testifies to the tragic failure of preventing unnecessary damage. That many human lives were lost under collapsed structures speaks for itself. Just as significantly, it is truly regretable, that school buildings were not utilized as shields against secondary damage in the post-tremor phase.

When a natural disaster strikes, school facilities act as very valuable regional facilities to support disaster-mitigating efforts. In countries with relatively well-organized disaster prevention regimes, school facilities are invariably designated by local municipalities as wide-area-coverage evacuation centers. Citizens affected by an earthquake or any other natural disaster will seek shelter at such locations. There is much merit to having such designated evacuation facilities to which disaster victims can be directed. For one thing, by having disaster-affected citizens gather in one place, it becomes possible to grasp the situation concerning the victims on the ground at an early stage. The municipal authorities concerned will thus be able to obtain a quick picture of the extent to which the affected citizens over whom they have jurisdiction have sustained physical injuries and property damage. They can then take indicated measures for providing appropriate medical treatments and health and sanitation management, as well as put procedural measures on the fast track toward fulfilling the requirements for the application of disaster-related laws concerning the restoration of normal life. The next step is the post-disaster formation of a community based on the idea of mutual help. In many cases, vulnerable people, especially the aged population, are apt to be exposed to a severe post-disaster psychological shock which will prove extremely stressful for their health. Those living close to them must provide support for such people with little disaster resistance. In Japan, when a large-scale natural disaster breaks out, portable telephone companies launch their disaster victims' message board service. This system makes it possible for people in and around disaster-affected areas to post appropriate messages regarding their safety or other messages which can be retrieved on the inquirers' terminal monitors.

KEY POINT

When a large-scale earthquake strikes, secondary damage is determined by where the tremor-affected people happen to be immediately following the tremor.

Recommendations

The government must:

- Designate large and sturdily built (public) school facilities as wide-area-coverage evacuation centers for use when a large-scale natural disaster occurs. It will also be necessary to secure access routes to insure that the evacuation centers can function effectively;
- Keep area residents informed of the evacuation centers that are ready for use in case of an earthquake-generated emergency.

Risk and Crisis Management for Daily Life: Cases 28–62

Case 28

Why Everyone Must Take Precautionary Measures

Things that are unlikely to happen actually do happen in an emergency. If you accept it as your fate and do not take any precautionary measures or preemptive steps, crisis management will fail.

There are three different attitudes toward **contingencies**.

The first is the most passive. You accept it as your fate and see taking any precautionary measures or preemptive steps as futile. Eighty-eight percent of the people who died in the Great Hanshin-Awaji Earthquake were victims of collapsed houses and buildings. In a contingency, an unlikely event happens in a very short period of time. The difference between life and death lie in the first several tens of seconds to several minutes after the earthquake occurred. Fatalistic people would have done very little to change the outcome.

The second is more pro-active. You try to improve your chances of survival in an emergency rather than leave it up to fate by preparing yourself with a contingency planning manual and making a list of things that should be done in various emergencies.

The third is the most pro-active approach. You not only try to identify the fundamental causes of natural and man-made disasters and prepare for various emergencies, but also try to predict their occurrence and address the causes.

There is some sense in each approach, but we think the third one is best. We believe taking the most pro-active approach is our duty as rational human beings.

Granted, people are busy with their daily lives. Without conscious effort, contingency planning will always take a back seat to the work at hand which, while requiring immediate attention may not be as consequential. Unless one overcomes this tendency perpetuated by inertia, the fatalistic approach becomes prevalent. Consequently, it results in a failure to take precautionary measures to guard against and prepare for emergencies.

KEY POINT

One should not put off until tomorrow what can be done today; do all that is humanly possible and let God take care of the rest.

Recommendations

Everyone should:

1. Inspect their home for vulnerabilities, such as its seismic adequacy;
2. Apply stopgap measures after the inspection;
3. Apply permanent measures at the earliest opportunity.

Why We Need to Repeat Simulated Experiences

It is not easy to sufficiently envisage an unexpected event that could occur in an emergency or have an opportunity to simulate the experience. This is where crisis management often fails.

Contingency planning manuals specify how to respond to various natural and man-made disasters. Yet there are limitless possibilities for the ways in which things could happen in a disaster.

For example, most manuals have a list of instructions in case of an earthquake as follows: turning off gas at the main and circuit breakers, getting out of a shaky house as soon as possible, and going to the designated evacuation facility.

If the disaster is mild enough for people to be able to follow the instructions in the manuals, there is no problem. However, if the earthquake is severe, you might not be able to walk to where the main gas valve is. Or, if the earthquake happens at night, the first challenge would be to locate a flash light in the darkness. Even if you manage to turn off the gas, can you easily get outside the house? Or is it feasible for you to get to the evacuation center? There are so many possibilities that **may not go according to what is stated in a manual**.

To overcome this problem, you need to document what to do in each situation in further detail. When doing this, it is important to devise a plan for a scenario where, for some reason, you cannot move around freely.

If you take the attitude that conceivable emergency situations are limitless and too numerous to catalog, then, contingency planning will fail. If you make an ongoing effort to identify potential problems and develop countermeasures, it will improve your chances of survival in an emergency.

KEY POINT

There is no perfect contingency planning manual. It is important to keep improving it through continuous effort.

Recommendations

Everyone must:

1. Repeatedly participate in simulated experiences;
2. Keep cataloging hypothetical scenarios of emergency situations.

When Knowledge Is Not Enough

After reading a disaster survival manual, you may think that you know full well what to do and how to respond in a time of disaster; however, crisis management may still fail.

A contingency survival manual can be a very useful source of information. However, it is a mistake to think that you are fully prepared for contingencies after just reading one or two of them.

After reading a manual, if there are things you have not put into practice yet, you should do so immediately. For example, bolting furniture to the wall or post, keeping a flashlight by your bedside, and hanging an emergency backpack inside the house near the front door are some of the things that you can easily prepare for.

Unfortunately, there are many things that are beyond **our personal capabilities**. For example, if you wish to have an additional emergency staircase built at your condominium, you would have to go to the condo management committee to have it approved first. It could take a long time to have your request implemented. Under ordinary circumstances, it is probably unlikely to happen.

Even if you scale down the scope of the project and request to have the staircase rail reinforced to increase its safety in an emergency, people who live on the lower floors might not agree that it is important.

With larger issues, such as the addition, expansion or improvement of evacuation facilities, it would take an enormous amount of time and effort on your part as you will need to mobilize local or state government.

Thus, even if you have the knowledge of what to do to prepare for emergencies, you might not be able to implement desirable measures before the next disaster occurs.

KEY POINT

Knowing what to do to prepare for emergencies is one thing, and taking necessary steps is quite another.

Recommendations

Basic steps in preparing for a disaster are to:

1. Bolt furniture to the wall or post;
2. Keep a flashlight by the bedside;
3. Keep an emergency backpack by the bedside or inside the house near the front door.

How Knowledge Acquired by Experience is Superior

Some lessons about crisis management can only be learned by actual experience. However, unless we organize the knowledge acquired from our own experience, crisis management will fail again.

There are many books, newspaper articles and TV reports written by and about people who have actually experienced disasters. It is very important to systematically organize lessons learned from these experiences.

We need to absorb relevant knowledge about disaster preparation from various sources (e.g. how to maintain lifeline utilities, prepare an emergency kit, ensure communications means and evacuate from a house in an emergency). The knowledge needed covers a wide range of topics at various levels for an individual household, neighborhood, district, region to nation.

For example, one of the suggestions on how to communicate at a time of emergency is to "always carry around coins that can be used to make a phone call." This is based on the assumption that one will need to use a public telephone.

In an attempt to rescue a person out of a collapsed house, you could actually do the person more harm by cutting off a pillar with a saw. Rather, it might be better to give the saw to the trapped person and let him/her cut a safer section for themselves. Also, if you can find a suitable pan nearby, it is a good idea to give it to them to put on their head for protection. The ability to improvise like this is an important skill to have during an emergency.

It is imperative that we accumulate **practical knowledge** about how to respond to various emergency situations.

KEY POINT

We can never learn enough about crisis management from actual experience.

Recommendations

Everyone should:

1. Always have coins available for an emergency phone call.
2. Be prepared to improvise and locate other people to assist you in order to rescue someone out of a collapsed house.

What to Do If a War Breaks Out While in a Foreign Country

If you face the looming threat of war while in a foreign country, you should leave the country as soon as possible. Otherwise, it might be fatal if you move around unnecessarily.

If the country you are visiting becomes embroiled in a war, you should try to get out of the country as soon as possible. However, it is not always easy to make a plane reservation under such circumstances because many flights are cancelled, restricted or fully booked.

When flying is not possible, evacuate to a neighboring country by train, ship or bus. According to Mr. Hisayoshi Tsuge (1994), "a taxi is the best choice if traveling by land and if no other more convenient transportation means are available." Because taxi drivers have thorough knowledge of the local area, they could be a great help as long as you can communicate with them.

Therefore, if you find a good taxi driver, you should use them on a regular basis and get to know them well before a time of crisis. When leaving the country by taxi, it would be better if you can find a friend to ride with to avert danger on the way.

If you decide it is too difficult or dangerous to leave the country, however, you should relocate yourself to a relatively safe place, such as a reputable hotel or your government's embassy or consulate. After moving to a hotel, stay inside and keep a low profile until the situation stabilizes, particularly if there are many people from adversarial countries staying there.

Follow the instructions of the hotel manager or employees. Do not place your head out of a window, or you might become a sniper's target. By the time street-by-street fighting starts, it is not unusual that gunmen will be put in place at the top of buildings, on street corners and the inside of main buildings.

KEY POINT

Wise men prepare for war in times of peace. (Homer, *Satire*)

Recommendations

If the country you are visiting is threatened by war:

1. Leave the country by plane as soon as possible;
2. Take a train, bus, or ship, if you cannot get a plane;
3. Use a taxi if it is available, and depending on circumstances.

What to Do If You Get Caught in an Emergency Abroad

During overseas trips, there are many possibilities for emergency situations to arise. Remember not to take unnecessary risks in a foreign country, or you might get into serious trouble.

It is important to keep in mind that during overseas trips an emergency could occur as early as the moment you land at an airport.

In fact, that is what happened to someone when he traveled to Israel and arrived at Tel Aviv Airport in 1972. Unfortunately, it was shortly after a shooting incident at the airport perpetrated by the Japanese Red Army terrorist group. Consequently, he had to undergo a thorough inspection of all his belongings as well as a strip search and extensive interrogation.

There was clear evidence of a shooting at the airport. Since he boarded the plane in New York, the likelihood of his involvement with the incident was rather slim. Still, since he was carrying a Japanese passport, it was understandable why they needed to investigate him as a potential member of the terrorist group.

After the rigorous body search and interrogation, the inspector apologized to him, but told him that he had no other choice under the circumstances. Although he was disconcerted about having to go through this unexpected situation, he expressed his sincere condolences for the victims and their families.

But what should you do if you are mistaken as a terrorist?

When a customs officer asks you questions, you could potentially get yourself into more trouble by trying to answer them yourself. It may be better to present yourself as not being able to understand the officer and not answer questions. You should request an interpreter and buy time to collect your thoughts.

If you understand why you are being detained and are absolutely confident about your innocence with respect to the allegations, you should ask them first to contact your **government's outpost agency**, such as an embassy or consulate, to request a representative to aid in your defense. If possible, you should contact them yourself and explain the situation clearly to see if the matter could be resolved immediately.

KEY POINT

As it is a crime to disturb the peace when justice rules, it is also a crime to hold on to peace when justice is about to be destroyed. (Pascal, *The Pensées*)

Recommendations

Should you be mistaken for a terrorist by the immigration staff at a foreign airport:

1. Buy time by declining to answer questions;
2. Request an opportunity to contact your government's outpost agency.

What to Do If You Get Arrested While Abroad

Imagine this scenario. After arriving at a hotel in a foreign country, you decide to walk into town. Suddenly, you are mistaken as a wanted person by the police and arrested. If you respond or act carelessly, it could cost you your life.

This is definitely a case of personal contingency. How should you respond in such a situation? If you are of the same nationality and resemble the wanted person in appearance, it is potentially even more complicated.

In such a case, it is important to **avoid answering questions unnecessarily on your own**. You could potentially say things to make yourself look more suspicious.

If the police ask you what you are doing and if you happen to have your passport with you, you should give them the flight number and arrival time of your plane at your destination. Then, explain that you arrived at a local hotel just a short while ago and came out to explore the town.

But they might not believe you if you left your passport in the safe deposit at your hotel. So, it might be better to say you got lost. But if the police keep asking you more questions, you should ask them to contact **your government's outpost agency** or ask for permission to contact the embassy or consulate yourself.

Hopefully, officials from the embassy or consulate will explain to the police on your behalf or you could travel there together to clear up any suspicions.

KEY POINT

It is important to carry around the contact information of your government's outpost agencies in foreign countries while traveling abroad.

Recommendations

Should you be arrested by mistake in a foreign country:

1. Request an interpreter;
2. Try your best to contact your government's outpost agency.

How to Avoid Terrorist Bombing Attacks

While indiscriminate terrorist attacks happen suddenly and take us by surprise, bombing attacks sometimes have warning signs.

On 7 July, 2005, a series of **bomb explosions** occurred on the London Underground trains and a London bus. Since the incidents occurred during the morning rush hour when many people were using public transportation, casualties were extensive. The bombings reportedly killed at least 40 people and injured more than 350 others. On 21 July, 2005, a second series of three failed bomb attacks took place on the London Underground. In response to these terrorist attacks, the Department of Homeland Security tightened security at mass public transport systems and U.K.-related facilities in the United States. These attacks occurred while the **September 11th Terrorist Attacks in the United States** in 2001 were still fresh in people's minds — they were stunning for their magnitude and audacity.

Terrorist acts include **suicide bombing, assassination, hijacking, bombing**, and **abduction**. Commercial airplanes and other public transportation systems are often targets of these attacks. Terrorists indiscriminately attack both political figures and private citizens.

What can travelers do to avoid an unexpected terrorist bombing attack? There are two points to consider here.

The first is that an al-Qaeda group was involved in these attacks. Al-Qaeda tends to launch multiple attacks on public transportation systems during rush hour when a political event is being held. (In this case, it was the G8 summit.) You should be extremely cautious if some international political or economic event is scheduled in the area you are visiting.

The second point is that this incident involved a series of bombings. Because they were set in public areas, there was a chance some people could have spotted them. If you see someone or something suspicious in a public place or transportation facility, you should report it to police or security right away.

KEY POINT

While traveling abroad, it is very important to pay attention to your surroundings in order to detect any potential threat.

Recommendations

Ministry of Foreign Affairs of Japan, "Q&A; Measures against terrorist explosions for Japanese/Japanese corporations in the process of going international" (Abstract from pp. 11–12)

1. What should you do to avoid getting involved in bombing attacks?

    1.1 Avoid going to an area where random bombing is occurring.
    1.2 Avoid going to a place which is at risk of becoming a target of terrorist bombing. If you must go, at least avoid the time of day when the random attacks tend to occur.
    1.3 When using an airport, avoid going near check-in counters unnecessarily, as they often become a target of terrorist attacks.

2. How should you respond in case you encounter a bombing incident?

2.1 If there is a bomb explosion in the vicinity:

2.1.1 Get down on the ground as soon as you hear an explosion (since there could be a second detonation).

2.1.2 If you are pushed down to the ground by an agitated crowd, hunch over with your knees pressed to your chest and minimize your personal injury by remaining still until the stream of panicked people calms down.

2.2 If you are buried under rubble by an explosion:

2.2.1 Don't light a match or cigarette lighter.

2.2.2 Don't move around unnecessarily.

2.2.3 Cover your mouth with a handkerchief to prevent the inhalation of noxious dust.

2.2.4 Let rescue workers know where you are by tapping a pipe with a hard object. (Be careful not to cause the rubble to collapse.).

2.2.5 Don't shout unless necessary as it could cause you to inhale noxious substances.

Note: The recommendations in this case were translated by the translator by referring to Akira Ishikawa and Atsushi Tsujimoto (2006), *Risk and Crisis Management 99*, Shumpusha Publishing, pp. 87–88. Ishikawa and Tsujimoto's article was based on "Q&A: Measures Against Terrorist Explosions For Japanese/Japanese Corporations In The Process Of Going International", Ministry of Foreign Affairs, Japan, pp. 11–12. Therefore the English translation of the recommendations was not formally announced from the Ministry of Foreign Affairs, Japan. If you need to confirm the exact English translation, please check with the Ministry of Foreign Affairs.

What to Do If You Find an Intruder in Your Hotel Room (1)

It is the first day of your overseas trip. You arrive at a hotel in the evening and go out for dinner and a short walk in the neighborhood. You decide to go to bed early so that you can rest up for the next day. You are awakened by a noise in the middle of the night. To your dismay, there is an intruder in your room. In this case, don't leap into action as it could cost you your life.

There are several possibilities why an **intruder** can have access to a locked hotel room.

It is not uncommon even in famous hotels that the burglar is an accomplice with a hotel bell captain or clerk. Most likely, he was given a copy of the key to your room with which he could easily enter if you did not lock the dead bolt from inside. To make matters worse, a master burglar can cut the door chain without making any noise.

Another possibility is that the burglar was already inside your room when you checked in. This is more risky for the burglar, but it is not impossible if he somehow knew you were going out soon after checking in and dropping your luggage. For example, if you are in a tour group, all the activities are usually scheduled in advance. So, the burglar may know that you will not have too much time to spend in the room after checking in.

At any rate, it is in the middle of the night and the burglar is standing by your bedside. If you make an unwise move, it could cost you your life. Also, you need to remember that you are likely to be fatigued from a long journey and jet lag and might not be able to move as quickly as usual.

In such a case, if you are awakened and asked for money, do as you are told. If the burglar tries to attack you with a knife or other weapon, you will need to fight off the attacker by using the pillow or comforter as a shield.

The critical point here is whether you can reach an **emergency buzzer** or **emergency communication unit**, with which every room should be equipped. Thus, you should make a point of checking where these devices are located as soon as you walk into your room after checking in.

KEY POINT

After checking in, make a point of locating the telephone, emergency buzzer, and emergency exit and staircase.

Recommendations

When staying in a hotel abroad:

1. Check where the emergency exit and staircase are located;
2. Check where the emergency communication unit is located;
3. Check to see if there is a safe deposit in your room.

Case **37**

What to Do If You Find an Intruder in Your Hotel Room (2)

You manage to reach and press the emergency buzzer. The siren goes off loudly and the flustered invader tries to escape hastily. Even at this point, it is too risky to pursue and attempt to wrestle him to the floor.

When I was living in New York City some 30 years ago, there was an incident in which a Japanese young man got stabbed to death on Houston Street in the City. He reportedly held a judo black belt.

In another case, there was a supermarket robbery in Tokyo where a university student was stabbed to death in 1985. He was trying to help catch a robber, but the fleeing person unexpectedly launched a lethal counterattack.

There are numerous cases where people pursuing thieves were **counterattacked and killed**. These incidents happen suddenly and do not give people much time to think. In many cases, the chasers engage the robbers without taking time to discern whether they are armed.

In this kind of situation, there is no guarantee that you will be able to catch the robber unless you are undoubtedly much stronger than him. It can be very risky particularly if the robber is working as part of a group.

When attempting to catch a robber, first discern **whether he is alone**. Second, try to gain control by using some tool such as a baseball bat, rod or broom, then make him stand facing the wall with both his hands on it, and check **whether he is armed**. Finally, kick him in the side and knock him unconscious before conducting a body search (H. Tsuge (1994). *Survival Bible*, p. 69 Hara Publisher).

If he tries to run away, chase him but maintain a distance of about 5 to 10 meters between the burglar and yourself. If he speeds up, you should speed up, too. Don't ever put your neck on the line by taking too much risk.

KEY POINT

When a situation calls for an instant reaction, overestimating your own abilities could bring on a disaster.

Recommendations

When attempting to catch a robber:

1. First, you need to prevent him from attacking you;
2. Next, determine whether he is armed. If he is, try to disarm him;
3. Report to the closest law enforcement authority.

Case **38**

How to Respond to a Medical Emergency Abroad

Mr. A developed appendicitis while he was on a field trip to a developing country. A contingency planning manual in the particular country had a list of local doctors and their contact information. It is important to remember, however, there are cases in which following a manual may not be the best course of action. Without appropriate measures, the situation could become life-threatening.

Mr. B, an overseas representative office manager in the country who took care of Mr. A's case, decided that it would not be a good idea to send him to a local medical institution for an operation, considering the level of the medical care system and poor hygiene in the country. Instead, he decided to airlift Mr. A to a hospital in the neighboring country, C, which had a more advanced medical system and better sanitary conditions.

One of the critical points in this case was whether Mr. A was able to withstand an airlift. Mr. B called a medical professional in the home country for advice and they jointly decided airlifting Mr. A to Country C would be the best course of action. Thanks to the wise judgment of Mr. B, Mr. A received appropriate treatment during a short hospital stay, and was also able to fulfill the objective of his field trip with just a few extra weeks added to his itinerary.

Mr. B said, "If we had followed the manual currently under development, it could have become a serious life-threatening situation."

The lesson to be learned from this experience is that an **emergency manual** is never a final product as it needs constant improvement and revisions.

If Mr. B had rigidly believed that he would be fulfilling his responsibilities as long as he followed the manual, then he could not have taken these kinds of emergency measures. He was able to make a good decision because he took many factors into careful consideration, such as the condition of the patient's illness and his potential recovery.

KEY POINT

When dealing with a medical emergency abroad, we need to be able to respond flexibly according to circumstances. Strictly following a manual does not always produce the optimum results.

Recommendations

1. We must keep improving and revising a crisis management manual for emergency purposes in a foreign country.
2. When addressing an emergency procedure for a case not documented in the manual, follow the advice of an expert or use your own common sense.

Why Analysis of Real-life Experiences are Needed

To step up contingency planning, diligently gather real-life experiences from people who have actually encountered various emergency situations themselves. Then, analyze them from major angles, gathering and summarizing the lessons to be learned.

Whether or not one has actually experienced emergency situations fundamentally affects how one would draw up a contingency planning manual.

Mr. Kazuhiko Arano wrote a book about his personal experience of the Great Hanshin-Awaji Earthquake, *108 Lessons from a Magnitude-7 Earthquake* (Avano, 1995). In his book he vividly recounted his experience of the earthquake from his residence in 11th floor a 14-story condominium on Port Island in Kobe.

He gives us many cautionary lessons about customary practices, some of which would not occur to people who do not have previous disaster experience: "The bathroom is not safe" (Lesson 10), "Don't rush down the stairs because strong aftershocks may cause you to lose your footing and fall" (Lesson 22), "Don't put a chest of drawers or wall-type air conditioner in the bedroom. They could fall down on you while you are asleep" (Lesson 24 and 25). It is easy to "keep a flashlight or lighter at one's bedside." However, it is not easy to remember to "**make sure there is no smell of gas before lighting a cigarette lighter**" unless we train ourselves to pay attention to details on a routine basis during ordinary times.

In addition, it is not easy to remember to "call somebody to let them know that you are okay before evacuation" unless you keep your composure in the event of an emergency.

Personal disaster experiences contain many valuable lessons we can learn from. These include lessons that could make a life-or-death difference, and avoid obstructing evacuation activities and causing parents and relatives great anxiety. It is important to work out these countermeasures during ordinary times.

KEY POINT

Nobody is wise enough to learn from other people's experiences. Their failure should be a warning to us. (*The Book of Han*, compiled by Ban Gu)

Recommendations

The best way to learn from real experiences is to:

1. Analyze as many personal experiences as possible to prepare for emergency situations.
2. Draw lessons from a comprehensive analysis of real-life experiences.
3. Imagine unforeseen situations and develop countermeasures.

How to Prepare for Emergencies on a Routine Basis

People are becoming more indifferent to society in a fast paced world. As social apathy and a sense of individual powerlessness become pervasive, the probability of failure becomes higher during crisis management.

British journalist Hadfield (1995), presented in his book these results from a survey taken by Japan's General Administrative Agency in 1983:

- Only 23 percent of professional (bus, taxi and truck) drivers knew what to do in the event of a major earthquake.
- Only nine percent of the professional drivers knew that seven expressways in the Greater Tokyo Area leading to the central city would be closed to regular vehicular traffic when a major earthquake occurs.
- To make matters worse, 68 percent of the residents in Tokyo are totally unprepared for earthquakes.

I checked with several friends and acquaintances and only one was well-prepared for an emergency evacuation. Furthermore, while doing research for this book, I talked to many professionals (e.g., technical personnel, politicians, government employees in charge of disaster prevention) and only one had taken any steps, although very rudimentary, to prepare for an earthquake.

There may have been a slight change in people's attitudes over the past decade, due to the frequent occurrence of natural and man-made disasters since the Great Hanshin-Awaji Earthquake in 1995. Yet, life in Tokyo seems very peaceful, at least on the surface. People seem to have totally forgotten what had happened after the great Kanto Earthquake in 1923: the raging firestorms that incinerated 140,000 people; the tragedy that claimed as many as 40,000 lives at the Army Parade Ground in Hifukusho-Ato region of Tokyo, which ironically was a designated emergency evacuation location; and the ferocious fire that jumped across the 200-meter wide Sumida River.

If people are too busy pursuing careers or keeping up with the latest fads, as they were in 1923, they have learned nothing about crisis management from their own history of disasters.

KEY POINT

If one cannot remember the past, one is destined to repeat it.

Recommendations

1. Everyone ought to make adequate preparations for emergency evacuation on a routine basis;
2. If you do not think you are well-prepared for a disaster, particularly an earthquake, start taking steps now.

Case 41

Why Portable Toilets Are Essential

Along with gasoline, disposable diapers, and portable gas burners (voted the most valuable item in a survey of victims of the Great Hanshin-Awaji Earthquake), "port-a-potties" (portable toilets) are turning out to be a necessity everyone should have handy during a disaster.

In *Surviving a Magnitude 7 Earthquake — Lessons Learned by a Doctor from a Tremor-Stricken Zone* (2003, pp. 89–90) published by Shoden-Sha in its "Shinsho" (New Books) series, Dr. Koji Tamura, who has survived two magnitude 7 earthquakes, writes that it is not always unconditionally necessary to stock up on foodstuffs and drinking water, which are unfailingly included in the common list of emergency supplies to be kept in stock.

According to the doctor's experience and research, the **48 hours following the earthquake** constitute the dividing line between life and death, and help would begin to be extended from all over the country past this time frame. In fact, following the Great Hanshin-Awaji Earthquake as well as the Chuetsu (Niigata) Earthquake, rescue teams arrived at the afflicted areas within 48 hours.

Since it is unlikely that we who live in this age of gluttony would starve to death in 48 hours, Dr. Tamura recommends a portable toilet as a more important emergency supply item than foodstuffs or beverages. One can tolerate hunger for one or two days, but not control one's bowel movement. So the portable toilet is of great utility and importance.

All types of portable toilets and emergency handy toilets are offered by department stores, Tokyu Hands (DIY stores) and other outlets that carry anti-disaster commodities. They vary in price, shape and size from a low 300 yen to 10,000 yen and up, and from handy-type goods to products featuring odor-killing chemical formulations and carrying cases.

A handy-type portable toilet is foldable and can easily be placed in a standard-sized traveler's bag and is very reasonably priced at about 500 yen. Lightweight portable toilets are convenient for care-giving use, use in traffic congestion, use on board a yacht or cruiser and cost about 1,000 yen. Products that stand up to use on a trip or in disaster-stricken situations go for about 1,700 yen.

A sturdier model, measuring 34 cm in height, 32 cm in width and 37 cm in depth, with a deodorant and a fecal matter storage bag, costs over 10,000 yen.

How useful a given product is cannot be determined without concrete information about the user's preference, purpose of use, etc., but all the same, a product of this kind will count as an essential item in situations resulting from a disaster and other emergency situations. To the extent that it tends to be overlooked, it is important that it be consciously included in the standard list of emergency supplies.

Key Point

A disaster, wherever or under whatever circumstances it strikes, generates unexpected necessities.

Recommendations

1. One should ordinarily, make a point of assuming the scenario of a disaster, and have a set of emergency necessities in place.

2. With the emergency supplies in place, take another look at your preparedness in the light of disaster situations in other areas.

Note:

It might be additionally noted that heating can become more important than food, especially in winter, as did happen at the time of the Chuetsu Earthquake with many disaster-stricken people with no other means of moving about than their automobiles. We are reminded in this connection that an emergency supply of blankets and warm clothes should always be kept in each family car. Also, public toilet facilities are generally in short supply, making disposable diapers for infants and elderly people an additional required emergency supply item.

Case **42**

How Typhoon Psychology is Fatal

The Great Kanto-Tokai Earthquake is the name for the major tremor considered certain to strike the southern Kanto Plain and its environs, but no one knows when it will happen. The fundamental issue here is how, in preparation for the disaster, each and every inhabitant of this country is to overcome the so-called "typhoon psychology." Doing nothing about it is certain to make a big fiasco of contingency plans and crisis management schemes.

Typhoon Psychology was the expression used by former United States Ambassador to Japan Edwin Reischauer, in referring to Japanese indifference to crisis management as it related to earthquake survival and other coping measures.

He was of course symbolically referring to the Japanese behavior of relegating to oblivion anything not worth remembering. When a typhoon warning is issued, the Japanese worry greatly that the typhoon may hit the area where they live and incur immeasurable damage and losses. But they know that, once the typhoon threat is gone, the weather will recover as though the rainstorm brought on by the marauding typhoon had never been a reality and that they can look forward to a cloudless, blue sky, clear air and a refreshing, life-giving sun. All typhoon-related thoughts are wiped out from their minds until the next typhoon arrives.

Given such escapism in a culture where commuters crushed on trains and lost in the pages of *manga* (comic) books and vulgar tabloids, or the same commuters with their eyes stuck on a pin ball's movement in a *pachinko* (pin ball) parlor for hours after a repetitive workday, or seeking refuge in the pleasures of inebriation, crisis management will be increasingly ignored.

If anyone has time for these leisurely pursuits, he should make time to deepen his knowledge about the Great Hanshin-Awaji Earthquake or the Great Kanto Earthquake.

He could visit a local facility such as a disaster prevention center or a showroom of Tokyo Gas where **earthquake are offered** and **life saving drill simulations or earthquake disaster prevention/survival videos are available** for viewing or renting. A little conscious effort on the part of every citizen will make all the difference in improving the overall effectiveness of crisis management.

KEY POINT

Of all battles, fighting against oneself is the most difficult, and there is nothing as gloriously victorious as overcoming oneself.

Recommendations

1. All citizens must make use of the nearest disaster prevention center and other facilities to bone up on prevention of causes for and alleviating the effect of typhoons and other natural disasters, and apply what they have learned.
2. With regard to earthquake disaster prevention, in particular, a daily habit of assiduous study is indispensable.

Why Specific Roles Should Be Allocated

When an earthquake warning is issued, the father (or mother) assumes at least two roles including one in the organization to which he or she belongs and another as the head of his or her household. The role to be played by each household member concerned should be clarified and understood by all ahead of the day being prepared for.

A **warning declaration** is an act of the State (Central Government) to alert the people to the probable imminence of an earthquake. But, at present, the only situation to which the issue of such a declaration applies is a major-scale earthquake of a magnitude class of 8 or higher, regarded as likely to hit the Tokai region.

In other words, no warning declaration will be issued for an earthquake of similar magnitude striking another region in the country.

Let us suppose that a warning declaration is issued early on Sunday morning. Since the father (or mother), the head of the household, and perhaps the grandparents and others, will be home, it will be a good time for them to get together and discuss among themselves what preparations they should start with and, in the eventuality of an emergency, in what order of priority they should act.

There is peace of mind in knowing that all members of the family are together and in direct communication with one another.

If, on the other hand, a warning declaration were to be issued in the afternoon on a weekday, the head of the household (father, mother, or both) would be away at work, and the child (or children) at school, each following the procedures stipulated in the crisis management manuals used by their respective organizations. If the aged grandparents were the only persons remaining in the house, their son, who would be the head of the household, would have to return home at once, but if he were in charge of anti-disaster readiness management at his work place, he would not even be able to do so.

Looking at the contingency from the standpoint of day of the week and hour of the day only is enough to show that crisis management is not at all straightforward and easy to handle. A crisis could not possibly be handled satisfactorily without a very clearly laid-out **allocation of roles** (or assignment of duties) prepared well in advance.

KEY POINT

For role allocation under a crisis management scheme to be effective, planning in advance with all factors taken into consideration is an absolute must, given that role assignments are subject to significant change depending on the prevailing situation on the ground.

Recommendations

1. Roles to be played within each household should be clearly defined in advance such that they will best meet the needs of typical situations.
2. Special considerations should go to care for elderly members of the family and infants.

Case **44**

How Specific Roles Should Be Allocated

When an earthquake warning is issued, there must already be a clearly defined role to be played by each individual concerned, several roles devolving upon one individual, if necessary.

We have already seen how the assignment of roles can vary significantly depending on the uniqueness of the situation associated with each earthquake, but broadly there are two categories of roles: multiple task, and single task.

An individual has **a multi-tasked role** when, at the time of the warning declaration, a head of a household must simultaneously discharge several roles (duties), for example, as a public figure, as a private individual, and as a neighbor. An individual has **a single-task role** when an individual discharges only one role either as a public figure or as a private individual.

If, following the issue of a warning declaration, the head of a household must take on the role of the chief of a neighborhood association or the head of his household, and not the role he will be assigned to at his work place, he will still be discharging a multi-tasked role. For this scheme to work, it is necessary, to have in place the methodology and scenario relating to when and how each role is to be discharged, well in advance of the emergency.

As touched on earlier, however, all concerned must be aware that the role allocations procedures vary in a major way depending on the given situation on the ground. But, at least in regards to the first thing to do, and in what order other steps should be followed, all parties concerned must be in agreement after all possible situations that might occur have been taken into consideration.

If an assigned role has not been duly fulfilled, who should take over the role as deputy should also be clearly stipulated.

This applies to the individual assigned to a single task as well. This is because, if, for example, a mother who has been assigned to the role of looking after all household-related matters sustains an injury herself, she would be unable to perform her assigned duties. If such a scenario were to happen, she would have to make inquiries about the order of actions to take, and precious time would be wasted. Thus crisis management would be doomed to fail.

KEY POINT

When designating roles, designate deputies (substitutes) as well.

Recommendations

In assigning roles:

1. Designate two or more deputies, with the deputization order indicated;
2. Organize everything so that, in an emergency, all persons concerned can spring into action according to a pre-established order of priorities.

Case **45**

How to Deal With Personal Risk (1)

For purposes of risk control in the context of individual-level crisis management, the undertaking will fail unless attention is paid to external hazards, physical hazards, discipline hazards and moral hazards.

To provide a clearer picture of the above four hazards, we will explain how they relate to the operation of an automobile.

An **exterior hazard** (a hazard of exterior origin) occurs when, for example, a storm of large hailstones surprises you while you are at the wheel (one of the authors actually just had such an experience while driving through the south of the United States), or a thick fog descends upon the stretch you are driving through (this one, too, was experienced by one of the authors in Seattle).

Small hailstones would present no problem, but being hit by table tennis ball-sized ingots of ice makes driving quite hazardous. You must find shelter as quickly as possible and take refuge.

An even nastier situation occurs when you are suddenly enveloped in a thick fogbank in the middle of driving on a freeway. You must of course turn on the fog lights, reduce your speed and attempt a quick exit from the freeway or pull over on the shoulder and stop.

A **physical hazard**, which is related to the external hazard in certain regards, occurs when, after rain in winter, the temperature goes down suddenly, and the road surface freezes up. When a situation such as this occurs, you must slow down to 20 to 25 km at most, driving with utmost care to prevent the vehicle from slipping and causing a serious accident.

A **discipline hazard** occurs when the motorist going at regular speed even though the road is in a condition such as just described or behaving in a reprehensible manner, sounding the horn at another car being driven with due care.

Moral hazards result from driving in a manner that inconveniences others, driving when we are sleepy, and using the horn merely by force of habit.

Dismissing out of hand or ignoring these hazards will eventually lead to dire consequences such as a big accident.

KEY POINT

Risk is not always of outside origin.

Recommendations

1. Risk at the individual level is of various types, and no risk should be treated as a one-dimensional issue.
2. In dealing with a risk at the individual level, what is of paramount importance is to nip in the bud.

Case 46

How to Deal With Personal Risk (2)

There are five important principles of personal risk control.

A maxim admonishes us: "Do not forget war in peace". This holds true as the first principle of **risk management** not only for individuals, but also for nations and international organizations. The basic formula for not allowing risk to materialize is to regard peace, or the prevalence of peace, as an anomaly, or as a temporary condition, and conduct your daily life on that basis.

The second principle is: "Do not take natural phenomena lightly." To live in harmony with nature is indeed desirable, but you should never forget that nature may turn into a threat at any moment. The autumn breeze that feels so soothing and pleasant to the skin can intensify into a typhoon, which can cause enormous damage. A snow-capped mountain in winter is beautiful to behold, but light-heartedly climbing it can launch a life-threatening avalanche.

The third principle is: "Do not violate the law." Going against the law is in itself an act of running a risk. To the extent that the maintenance of order forms a basis of the law, to go against it is to inconvenience others in one way or another, which, depending on the degree of the offense, increases the risk. And even if one escapes adversity once, it will come back later in the form of an accumulated, bigger risk.

The fourth principle is: "Acquire good manners, assimilate a wealth of common sense, and never run counter to them." When applied to driving a car, the force of this principle may become clearer: Do not sound your horn more than is necessary when you are not in a hurry. Do not drive at an alarmingly slow speed when on a freeway. Do not obstruct a car trying to pass you.

The fifth principle is: "Do not be too willing to do others a favor or make a promise too light-heartedly." If, without thinking too much, you become a guarantor for a friend, or borrow money to purchase an expensive piece of jewelry, or agree to its safekeeping, it can happen that you will end up deep in debt yourself, being unable to return the debt, or having the jewelry damaged, or having to compensate for letting it be stolen.

KEY POINT

For individual-level risk control, be especially mindful of never being too willing to do others a favor.

Recommendations

For self-preservation, one must:

1. Be prepared for the powerful forces of natural phenomena;
2. Not violate laws;
3. Not light-heartedly agree to be a guarantor for a friend.

Case 47

How to Prevent Fires at Home (1)

One household contingency is the hazard of a fire, which may be of external or internal origin. Small hazards, microscopic as they may appear, could, if not taken seriously enough, develop into an accident.

A fire is a major contingency which will involve not only your own home, but, depending on the direction of the wind or dryness of the atmosphere, possibly other people's homes as well.

It follows, then, that we must work out preventive measures to eliminate fire hazard factors, which may be divided into, for example, an **external factor** (hazard of external origin) and an **internal factor** (hazard of internal origin).

Hazards of external origin include arson, spontaneous ignition, induced fire, etc., which occur beyond our control. In these cases, little preparation can be done in advance by way of taking preventive measures.

Hazards of internal origin, on the other hand, can be classified into physical hazard, discipline hazard, and an ignorance hazard.

A **physical hazard** can start a fire when, for example, an oil-stained cloth is carelessly left lying near a stove, or other inflammable material nearby catches fire. A **discipline hazard** concerns cases in which someone recklessly throws away a lit cigarette, a smoldering match, etc., which sets fire to flammable material nearby.

An **ignorance hazard**, related to the discipline hazard in certain ways, causes a fire when someone neglects to completely put out the embers of a bonfire, or dozes off with the switch of the heater of a *kotatsu* (quilt-covered low table) on.

These are all cases in which major fires are caused by casual carelessness. In each case, a small bit of effort will prevent contingencies from flaring up. Carelessness and pranks are accomplices to fires in unpredictable places and times.

KEY POINT

Household fire prevention must be approached from the perspectives of external and internal hazards.

Recommendations

Every member in every household must remember:

1. Not to throw away lit cigarettes and matches without smuffing out the flame;
2. Not to smoke in bed;
3. To switch off all burning items before going to bed.

How to Prevent Fires at Home (2)

Post-earthquake fire prevention, in all organizations and households, requires the highest priority after the protection of lives.

The Great Kanto Earthquake of 1 September 1923 struck at noon and triggered a mega-conflagration which destroyed 90 percent of homes in Tokyo and 60 percent in Yokohama. Just under 90 percent of the dead were burn victims. The dead and wounded at the massively inflamed Honjo Army Clothing Depot alone numbered some 40,000.

The conditions surrounding the Great Hanshin-Awaji Earthquake were milder, striking as it did early in the morning, but the fires raging left and right that we witnessed were nothing short of unimaginable misery.

It is common now as a matter of course to **pull out plugs from power outlets** when a house is going to be unoccupied for an extended period or as soon as an earthquake hits. But at the time of the Great Hanshin-Awaji Earthquake disaster this was not in practice. Cases were reported of household items, such as toasters being left on and exposed overheated thermostats for tropical fish tanks, and fire. Home appliances designed to improve quality of life and foster peace of mind became sinister tools of destruction.

These and uncountable other episodes remind us that, even if all the electric plugs had been pulled out, it would have been impossible to eliminate other causes of fire such as short-circuited internal wirings igniting gas leaks. Even if we know that decoupling the master breaker is the most effective fire prevention solution, we are too accustomed to the comfort of convenience to turn it, especially in the midst of summer's heat or the biting cold of winter, unless a warning declaration has been issued.

Yet the loss of lives and assets to fire is simply too devastating. Each of us must continue to put into practice well-conceived crisis management measures to ensure we have not failed to learn from our tragic experience.

KEY POINT

Crisis management requires well-planned and preparation organization.

Recommendations

All households must remember to:

1. Pull out all power source plugs as soon as an earthquake strikes;
2. Disconnect toasters and other electrical appliances;
3. Decouple the master breaker.

How to Ensure the Safety of Your Infant

If you are going out with your spouse and leaving your infant at home, make sure that you have a reliable baby-sitter.

At the top of your what-to-do list for household crisis management are, unquestionably: **Fire prevention, anti-theft, and anti-earthquake measures**. These have significant impact on lives and assets.

But equally important priority must also be given to infant care. When a young couple contemplates going out, they should know that leaving their infant, or infants, at home alone is an extremely risky act.

First of all, there is no way of foreseeing the behavior of the infant left alone. Will they be turning on and off the gas valve? Will they be swallowing little toys, or falling from the veranda? There is no end to the possibilities of danger. Obviously infants will not know how to contact their parents or relatives in case of an emergency.

What is to be done in case of a fire or an earthquake? What if a burglar breaks in? It is not only what the infants may do that makes the situation risky, but we must also consider external risks. What if a visitor comes knocking on the door? To play it safe, the parents may feel compelled to lock the doors and windows from the inside and outside.

In such a situation, there is no safety assurance. Thus it is absolutely necessary to ask for help from a reliable acquaintance or hire a **baby-sitter** from a reliable source to look after the infant.

The risk that comes from such negligence is immeasurably cost-lier than that of securing help; to be clear-eyed about this to practice proper risk management.

KEY POINT

The risk from leaving an infant alone at home is too great.

Recommendations

1. If you are thinking of going out and leaving your infant at home, think again. By all means drop the infant off at a child care facility or similar establishment;
2. If you cannot do so, then forgo the trip.

Case **50**

How to Ensure Water Supply

If you neglect the water component of your crisis management, water being a critical lifeline, your crisis management will fail even if your contingency plan is without fault in other respects.

For a snapshot of how water shortage can affect people's lives, a cursory review of 1994 alone shows that almost 16 million across the nation were affected by water supply restriction, including supply interruptions. The City of Fukuoka, in particular, enforced water supply restriction for almost 10 months until May 1995.

In the days and weeks that followed the Great Hanshin-Awaji Earthquake in January 1995, 1.3 million households were affected by water supply interruptions and other inconveniences, partly because of damage to water mains and water purification facilities in nine prefectures (including two Fu's [Osaka and Kyoto]). Six weeks after the earthquake, more than 40,000 households in Kobe and other areas were still without water supply; it took an incredible three months before the service was finally restored.

Based on experiences such as this, the City of Fukuoka, following the **Great Water Shortage** of 1978, distributed to each household faucet-mountable water flow control devices while calling on all consumers to practice reuse of rainwater and treated sewage water.

The 1995 Water Resource White Paper carried an article describing how the Fukuoka Municipal authorities, to prevent water supply interruptions from occurring in elevated areas, divided the city into a number of sections in support of a technical solution that would equalize the water pressure for all sections.

As a result of this undertaking, the total hours of water supply interruption for 1996 went down by 40 percent compared to 1978 in spite of the fact that the precipitation for 1996 was 20 percent less than for 1978. Alongside Fukuoka, there are other places where equipment for making use of rainwater for flushing toilets and irrigation is being promoted.

Water resource crisis management, in the ultimate instance, focuses on two issues: how to deal with drought and ensure water supply during major earthquakes. All dedicated efforts to work out solutions with duly appropriated budgets deserve to be rewarded with the appropriate results.

If water saving efforts are relaxed to a mode dominated by the "water is free" mentality, both supplies of emergency drinking water and water reserves for fire fighting and fire prevention activities may eventually face resource shortfalls. We should never relax our grip on the understanding that crisis management starts with conservation of water resources.

KEY POINT

Water is one of our most important lifelines.

Recommendations

1. We must never stop conserving our water resources.
2. For water resources management to be complete, the twin pillars of drought control and maintaining water supplies during an earthquake will have to be securely established.

How to Maximize the Use of Flashlights

It is well known that a flashlight is an indispensable emergency item. But without having learned to make effective use of it, we cannot regard our contingency plan or crisis management setup as complete.

The **flashlight** is among the most widely used of emergency items. Flashlights must be instantly available for the eventuality of a major earthquake striking at night and leading to a power outage.

One good location to keep them is by the bedside (close to your pillow). Most emergency management manuals offer the same recommendation.

Always ensure a fresh supply of batteries so that the flashlight will light all the way from your house to the evacuation shelter.

During an outage in the night, you will have to look for your flashlight in the dark. You cannot afford to waste time by groping about in the dark for your flashlights where you think you have left them. In the meantime, you are exposing yourself to the danger of your house collapsing from an aftershock.

To avoid such a situation, one could be a little creative and **paint the flashlight a luminous colour**.

It will also be necessary to attach the flashlight with a strap such that it can hang from the neck. When you are seeking a way out of your house, removing heavy furniture, bits of collapsed walls and anything blocking your way, an encumbered pair of hands will determine how efficient you are.

Simple emergency items carry far-reaching implications for crisis management solutions. We must be clear about this when designing our contingency plan.

KEY POINT

The usefulness of a single flashlight has far-reaching implications for crisis management.

Recommendations

Remember to:

1. Keep your flashlights by your bedside;
2. Paint your flashlights with luminous paint;
3. Hang your flashlight by its strap around your neck at the first tremor and assume the worst scenario.

Case 52

Why the Need for Self-Insurance

The purchase of life insurance or loss insurance is integral to crisis management and contingency planning design. However, in view of rising insurance premiums, restrictions on underwriting and low insurance payments, alternative insurance solutions need to be considered.

The loss attributed to the Great Hanshin-Awaji Earthquake was estimated in one report to amount to ¥10 trillion, but the insurance money payable from the insurers was foreseen to total no more than ¥200 billion, which would cover a paltry two percent of the actual loss amount. This shows that **earthquake insurance** is practically useless, although it is supposed to be one of the reliable disaster lifelines.

It reflects the unwillingness of insurance companies to underwrite high-risk accounts in view of the fact that the earthquake occurrence rate in the Pacific Rim is very high.

To make matters worse, car insurers as well as fire insurers for offices and other categories raised their premiums in February 1995, with a general trend toward higher insurance premiums for more categories since. In the meantime, a Product Liability Act went into effect, triggering an up surge in the number of lawsuits against stockholder representatives and other parties.

This compels us to ask if there may be other insurance policies that can be assembled together for an alternative solution.

Shigeki Urashima, former Representative Executive of Risk Managers and Consultants Association of Japan, proposes a **self-insurance** scheme under which the business pools its insurance funds internally instead of paying the insurance premiums to an insurance company (*Ima-shiritai Kikikanri — Want to know Crisis Management now* 1995; p. 83)," The basic purpose of the proposed scheme is to reduce insurance cost by allocating reserve funds for self-protection. We must note that the traditional insurance paradigm is not the only option.

KEY POINT

Relying on insurance companies is not the only option.

Recommendations

1. Keep reinforcing your anti-litigation insurance measures.
2. Further consolidate your personal computer networking setup.
3. Bring your reporting mechanism up to date for data concerning victims' emergency contact information, new location, extent of damage sustained, etc.

How to Deal with Bankruptcy of Financial Institutions

With the increasing frequency of financial institutions filing for bankruptcy today, it is dangerous to entrust them with your financial resources without careful consideration.

There were premonitions of bankruptcy of Japanese financial institutions in the summer of 1995 and cases suddenly began cropping up.

Two failing Tokyo credit unions were among the first to file for bankruptcy, which were, in due course, followed by Cosmo Credit Union, Bank of Hyogo, Kizu Credit Union, Yamaichi Securities and Hokkaido Takushoku Bank (as they were called in their day). As more became known about these, their **sloppy and reckless management** in these financial institutions were brought to light.

Incidents resembling the late 1980s savings and loans scandal set off in the United States political shockwaves that began to occur in Japan. Financial institutions which had been operating under a convoy of anti-bankruptcy firewalls were affected. The authorities were compelled to acknowledge that financial institutions were fast looming as objects of great risk.

Loud calls have been made for financial institutions to reinforce their systems for responsibility and accountability, but that will not spell the end of the problem.

For a start, financial institutions must make a full disclosure of their management operations and strengthen their audit function. As is the practice in the United States there must be a system of credit rating and risk assessment. A process is urgently needed to commend managers for taking accountability for every stage of the risk management system.

It is becoming increasingly necessary for businesses and households to aggressively collect pertinent information on the financial institutions they have dealings with and subject to their **risk assessment**.

KEY POINT

There is a need to make information disclosure mandatory and reinforce risk management.

Recommendations

Financial institutions need to:

1. Disclose, as much as possible, their management operation;
2. Make the audit function independent, and reinforce it.

Case 54

How the Lifting of Payoffs Ban has Affected Risk

The payoffs ban was generally lifted as of April 2004. Deposits (savings) of individuals and businesses exceeding a set amount would no longer be completely guaranteed. The peace of mind which comes from knowing that the entire amount of a large deposit is guaranteed has been reduced to a memory of history.

The **payoff** is a system which guarantees the account holder a refund of up to ¥10 million in capital and any interest accruing to it when a financial institution goes bankrupt. All financial institutions subscribe to the Federal Deposit Insurance Commission as members, which pays the depositor an insurance settlement with the upper limit at a set amount when a bank declares bankruptcy.

Before the ban on payoffs was lifted, depositors were instructed to protect their interests by taking actions such as: "The depositor should not have an entire account exceeding ¥10 million deposited with any one financial institution, but rather to disperse his assets into smaller deposits with several different institutions — banks, credit unions, workers' credit unions, etc.", "If you have your assets deposited with a financial institution to which the payoff applies, split your assets between the joint account with a spouse and a parent-child joint account, each under a different account-holder's name," etc. From the viewpoint of "securing peace of mind," one could deposit assets in the **postal savings account** (with an upper limit of ¥10 million) which is completely guaranteed by the Government and to which the payoff does not apply.

The postal savings system conveniently provides ATM all over the country, and is truly a national bank. As a matter of fact, depending on the type of deposit, the interest from the post office is similar to a bank's. Moreover, unlike banks, the postal savings service does not charge an off-hours service fee for night-time or holiday use. It is frustrating to see a night-time handling charge debited from your account when you go to the bank at night because you work during the day; by contrast, the postal savings service enjoys a credibly "conscientious" and "reliable" image as a financial institution.

On 5 July, 2005, the Privatization of Postal Services bill, which primarily provided for the splitting of the Japan Post into four independent entities, was passed with the Liberal Democratic Party and Komeito Party accounting for the majority vote. Amid the privatization of postal and telecommunications services, the postal savings service stands to be privatized now that it has been stripped of the Government-backed guarantee (as of 24 July, 2005). The risk of its being exposed to the danger of bankruptcy will have to be reckoned with. A bulwark against payoff applicability has crumbled.

KEY POINT

Financial institutions are no longer bankruptcy-proof.

Recommendations

If you are a bank-account holder:

1   Try not to deposit more than ¥10 million with any one specific financial institution;
2   Disperse your assets into smaller deposits with several different institutions — banks, credit unions, workers' credit unions, etc.;
3   Split your assets between you and your spouse's joint account and a parent-child joint account, each under a different account-holder name, if you have your assets in deposits with a financial institution to which the payoff applies.

What Clothing and Other Personal Effects are Appropriate

To be emergency-ready, you must have clearly organized what type of clothing you should have on when evacuating at the time of a disaster. It is practically impossible, to be sure, to change into emergency clothing in an instant, and you may expose yourself to unnecessary risk by taking time to change.

The right attire can help you **survive a disaster**. The following list includes what you should have ready at all times:

1. **Helmet**, or any other disaster prevention headgear. Have one on even in summer. When passing by a building that has collapsed in an earthquake, you may have roof tiles, window panes, billboards, neon signs, etc., tumbling down or falling on you.
2. Use long sleeves and long trousers to minimize injury to exposed parts of your body. Avoid items made of chemical fiber because they are not fire-resistant and are low on moisture retention; and hence to be avoided especially in winter.
3. Shoes with as thick soles as possible are recommended. Shoes with regular soles do not provide enough protection against glass shards and other injury-causing pointed objects.

4. Gloves, especially **army gloves**, are indispensable for injury-preventing purposes. It is conceivable shards of glass and pieces of wood will be scattered in your way that cannot be picked up with bare hands.
5. **Diapers** and **sanitation articles**, the availability of which was very much appreciated at the time of the Great Hanshin-Awaji Earthquake.
6. It will be particularly worthwhile to carry a personal identification card, laminated or secured in a capsule, with data on address, name, gender, name of school (or place of work), contact information, blood type, age, date of birth, name of guardian (if a child), name of disease (if afflicted with a chronic disease), etc. Such cards too, should be made for children and old people who should carry them at all times.

KEY POINT

In readiness for an unexpected turn of events, emergency clothing should be prepared and kept available at all times.

Recommendations

1. In an emergency, wear a helmet or any other protective headgear even in summer.
2. Wear a long-sleeved coat and slacks, even in summer, to minimize exposed body parts.
3. As much as possible, wear shoes that are thick-soled and sturdy.

Case 56

What to Do In An Emergency When Driving or Using an Elevator

What is one to do if disaster strikes while driving a car or riding in an elevator?

Where we are and what we are doing when a disaster strikes forms the basis of how we deal with the crisis. To be emergency-ready, we must have thought through a wide variety of conceivable scenarios starting out with: At home, or at work? If at home, inside or outside the house? If outside, in the yard, or in the hall?

Suppose, for example, you are **driving a car when a major earthquake strikes**.

It is said that, driving becomes difficult at seismic magnitude 5 and impossible at 6, with the steering wheel quite out of control. If, therefore, a magnitude 6 tremor hits, you must pull over to the road's shoulder just as quickly as possible while maneuvering your car carefully so as to avoid other cars. The *Earthquake Disaster Prevention Handbook* (1995, printed by the Ministry of Finance Printing Office under the supervision of the Ministry of Internal Affairs Fire Service Agency Anti-Earthquake Disaster Measure Implementation Guidance Office) points out that you should avoid stopping your car in an intersection and pull into a parking lot nearby. This is to keep the middle of roads and intersections open for exclusive use by ambulances.   .

Once you are safely parked, you will want to turn on your car radio for the latest earthquake information. If you have to leave your car to walk to an evacuation destination, roll up all your windows to prevent flames from being drawn into the car; leave the ignition key in the switch, and exit without locking the doors.

What if you are in an elevator when the earthquake strikes? If the elevator is equipped with a device that automatically causes it to stop at the next level, quickly get off there; if not, push all the buttons, and get off on the storey where the elevator stops. If you are surprised by an earthquake when you are on a high floor, never use an elevator as a means of quick evacuation because **taking an elevator is too risky during an earthquake**.

KEY POINT

Once an earthquake hits, never run into an elevator.

Recommendations

1. If you are in an elevator when an earthquake occurs, quickly get off at the first stop.
2. If you are driving a car when an earthquake occurs, pull over to the road's shoulder as quickly as you can, taking care not to run into other cars, and leave the car there.

Case 57

Why the Need to Fall Back on "Self-Help" When Overseas

Coastal resort destinations in other parts of the world have been visited by large-scale tsunamis, and governments concerned have been installing tsunami early warning systems and consolidating their information communication systems for the benefit of tourists. But foundational crisis management in such situations is the need for the tourists to help themselves.

The lesson learned from the Sumatra Earthquake, which left uncountable lives and properties lost on an unprecedented scale in its aftermath, is that we must continue down the generations to tell, and have retold, the story of the utter horror of the havoc brought on by that tsunami and ourselves keep our sense of crisis alive from day to day. By repeatedly taking cognizance of and analyzing past damages, we will learn to foresee to some extent what measures we may for our self-protection. This is a point that hearkens to the heart of so-called **risk management** consciousness.

If we should be caught in a natural disaster such as a tsunami while overseas, what **optimum measures can we take to limit any damage we may suffer?**

Crisis management theory suggests three operational levels of help. **Self-help, mutual help, and public assistance.** "Self-help" means personally preparing for a disaster by stocking up on emergency shelter bags, securing emergency necessities, and confirming your familiarity with the evacuation route and emergency shelter location. It is expected that, if you are not wounded and are capable of moving about on your own, you should independently take quick action without waiting for a helping hand from public sources.

"Mutual help" functions among territorially-connected organizations such as self-governing disaster prevention groups, laterally-linked organizations such as volunteer groups, quasi-public organizations such as fire-fighting groups, flood prevention groups, etc. "Public assistance" refers to responsive action by government agencies.

Japan lacks accumulated know-how in dealing with the consequences of large-scale tsunami because the country has so far been spared such an experience. The Ministry of Land, Infrastructure, Transport and Tourism has announced that at the formal request of the Government of Thailand it is putting together a technical assistance package that includes such items as the laying of evacuation routes from tourist facilities and the development of evacuation manuals. It is a time-consuming undertaking to create a well-coordinated disaster-prevention-oriented community at an overseas tourist destination frequented by people with different levels of disaster experience and of different languages.

When visiting overseas tourist destinations, one should uphold a **spirit of self-help** and be alert at all times.

KEY POINT

Heaven helps those who help themselves.

Recommendations

1. The Ministry of Foreign Affairs, municipality representative offices overseas and travel agencies should compile hazard maps (disaster warning/prediction maps) for tourist destinations and provide outbound tourists with one each.

2. When visiting a tourist destination in a coastal zone overseas, bring along an emergency evacuation bag with minimum supplies of drinking water, food and other emergency items, and independently (or accompanied by the tour coordinator) confirm the evacuation route and the evacuation facility.

How Spyware Infects Your Computer

Not all software programs available on the Internet, which are downloadable free of charge, are beta-version products for customers to evaluate for performance and functionality.

When one of the authors was attending an information processing class at his university in 2003, many computers being used by the students were infected by a **computer virus** called Blaster Worm. At large was a malignant virus releasing attack data that took advantage of a vulnerable side of the Windows OS. The Windows OS would repeatedly end and restart, completely disrupting class work. The campus authorities immediately, banned all infested personal computers from connecting to the campus LAN and began putting virus eradication measures in place.

In recent years, **spyware**, which is virus-like in form, has been circulating *en masse*. More effort is now being poured into combating its activity. What makes dealing with spyware troublesome is that students with personal computers exposed to its effects tend to report it late because any actual damage sustained is not immediately obvious.

Unlike viruses, spyware is seldom destructive, nor does it ever if at all, show up as an infection. In most cases, its function does not go beyond collecting personal information about the user of the personal computer connected to the Internet environment or about the user's preferences, and may be said to represent primarily marketing research. Spyware is most often contained in **freeware**, **shareware** and **adware** (types of software products which the user can use free of charge in exchange for agreeing to the product carrying ads of commercial interests). There are also other products which are activated by the computer user simply browsing through specific websites.

It is difficult to counter these types of software as categorically, they cannot be treated as illegal. The creator of the software explicitly states in the **User Consent Form** that the product is a software program that incorporates spyware and that it is being offered for free use in exchange for the user's consent to the product such as it is, or the Agreement states that the product includes spyware in its software for marketing purposes.

KEY POINT

There is nothing as scary as *free of charge* when it comes to computer software.

Recommendations

1. Before using a free software product, read the user consent form carefully, and do not install it if you do not consent to any portion of the stated stipulations.
2. Install in your personal computer an anti-virus software program with a reinforced spyware detection function and a software program specifically designed to delete spyware.
3. Periodically update your Windows.

Why Internet Auctions are at Your Own Risk

An Internet auction is a form of transaction in which both seller and buyer can participate without complicated formalities, but because credit information concerning the seller is scarce, especially in individual-to-individual transactions, trouble may incur, more often than not.

The rapid sophistication of the Internet community is making life increasingly convenient. According to *Telecom Use Trend Survey for 2003*, the Internet-using population was 77.3 million strong (accounting for 60.6 percent of the population). Riding on the crest of such a trend, **Internet auctions** have sprung up as virtual market-places where shoppers can enjoy shopping without worrying about time and location restrictions or inconveniences.

At an Internet auction, the seller sells his or her "white elephants" (articles no longer needed by the seller), and the buyer closes the transaction at an agreeable price. Because the transaction procedure is easy and convenient, participants in such auctions are increasing in number very rapidly. But the transactions are rife with compli-cating factors such as "A notable self-identity concealing trend among the players is potentially problematic", "There is no specific commercial code applicable to Internet transactions between individuals", "Warranty for defective/broken merchandise is not clearly spelled out", etc. A pattern of transaction irregularities which is particularly harassing for the buyer is seen in the **fraudulent behavior of sellers**, with the buyer making claims such as "I have made the payment, but the promised merchandise has not been delivered." Among other frequently encountered examples of trouble are situations where credit information pertaining to the transactions is scarce, e.g., "The seller's contact information is fictitious", or "Title is ambiguous, and comments about merchandise are presented as an image". Other specific cases include such examples as "No image of merchandise", "Abnormal delay in shipment", "Refuses to disclose seller ID or contact information" (YAHOO! AUCTIONS, http:// auctions.yahoo.co.jp/).

To keep an eye on Internet-based commercial transactions, the Ministry of Economy, Trade and Industry, working with other interested entities, conducts **Internet Surf Day**. The aim is to check advertisements posted on the Internet for compliance with relevant laws and regulations, and if there is any violation of the Act on Specified Commercial Transactions, the violator will be subjected to administrative guidance.

Auction site operators, for their part, now display notices of prohibited behavior at the auction as well as trouble avoidance policy statements, and, additionally, ask users to inform the site operators of any auction ID's (merchandise submitter ID's) which seem to run counter to merchandise transaction guidelines.

Internet fraud prevention endeavors by both public and private sources notwithstanding, there seems no end to irregularities occurring. "What is important is not to jump at the first item that pleases your fancy, but to take a deep breath and act with due diligence: Do what you can do to verify that the seller is a credibly trustworthy merchant," says of *Tomomi Yoshida* (undergraduate student, Meiji University). This is a concisely stated, apropos piece of advice.

Ultimately, the problem with Internet auctions lies in the fact that "**credit-based merchandise transactions**" between individuals are taken for granted. The credit information pertaining to the merchants must naturally be provided by the merchants themselves, but it certainly devolves upon the buyer as well to do his or her due diligence with elaborate research for verification.

KEY POINT

Given that Internet auctions in many cases are where individuals (or individual business operators) sell merchandise, laws and regulations governing transactions with which businesses regularly comply are often only marginally applicable. This is a form of business which, by its very nature, definitely needs to build trust-based relationships in merchandise transactions. The seller will have to disclose clear and detailed information on the merchandise, contact method, and transaction method, while the buyer will have to conduct thorough research on the seller (as well as the merchandise offered) before participating in the auction at his/her own risk.

Recommendations

If you participate in Internet auctions:

1. Confirm the seller's explanations about the merchandise (condition of the product, shipment schedule, payment method, etc.);
2. Ascertain that the seller's physical address, contact information and email address are given;
3. Verify that the seller can be contacted using the given contact procedures;
4. Check if you are satisfied, with the seller evaluation information at the auction site;
5. Conduct research on the bank with which the seller has an account, the same seller's postal savings account and other relevant points;
6. Check to see whether the compensation package offered by the auction site is applicable to you, should you, be victimized by fraud.

Case **60**

How to Counter Phishing Fraud

Cases of fraudulent theft of personal information from the email environment for assets robbery ("phishing fraud") are increasingly frequent. Because the modus operandi is extremely sophisticated, utmost precaution must be exercised in online transactions.

In recent years, **phishing fraud** has been sweeping cyberspace with a vengeance. The word "phishing" is said to be a coinage/neologism derived from the combination of *"sophisticated"* and *"fishing."* Phishing mailings are most often delivered in the form of a spam (unsolicited commercial mail).

According to Anti-Phishing Working Group (APWG), the largest organization of its kind in the United States, the phishing sites reported for November 2004 numbered 1,707. The numbers are growing at an accelerated rate in the United States today, and it is feared that, in Japan, too, the number of victims is headed for an increase.

Phishing fraud operations are generally performed in the following manner: First, posing as an existing bank or credit card company, the operator sends off a camouflaged email rigged with link buttons. Because the domain name of the sender looks convincing enough as the name of a real corporation, the recipient, without thinking too much follows the instructions clicks on the link button. The window that pops up asks the recipient to enter his or her credit card number and secret number.

Anti-phishing measures are in place on the card issuer side as well. But in most cases, the targeted terminals are Internet-connected home computers with no security patch protection, and here the importance of a downstream defense mechanism is clearly evident.

KEY POINT

Phishing fraud is not perpetrated at a technological level which would allow it to automatically lift a reading of credit card numbers or secret numbers. What should be guarded against is lack of precaution on the part of the email recipient in light-heartedly invitation accepting senders of camouflaged emails.

Recommendations

All email users should:

1. Look out for the warnings and bulletins issued by APWG;
2. Refer any suspicious statement, looking like a fictitious bill or some fraudulent document, to the National Consumer Affairs Center of Japan or National Liaison Committee of Consumers' Organizations;
3. Contact the sender to confirm contact information (address, telephone number) his or her;
4. Confirm the "Received from" field which should identify the SMTP server the mail header would have come through (sloppily sent phishing mails can sometimes be identified through this procedure);
5. Close the browser if the address of the sender you accessed by clicking on the link button looks patently suspicious.

Case 61

How to Protect Yourself Against Credit Card Skimming (1)

The conventional type of credit card-related damage has for the most part been accounted for by card theft or loss and, in more serious cases, fraud by card forgery; but more recently there have been increasing numbers of cases reported in which card forgery is performed by a method known as *"skimming"* *with the card owner being unaware of it.*

In June 2005, **a massive amount of customer information leaked** out of the information system of an outside service provider hired by the major American credit card company, **MasterCard International**. Card issuer companies directly contacted their customers, re-issued them new ID numbers and sent them replacement cards. In Japan, cards for use associated with physical distribution channels, were said to have been forged based on the data leaked and reportedly used for purchases at home electric appliance stores and elsewhere. This incident exposed the weakness of today's technological society.

In online shopping, once the shopper makes a purchase, his or her credit card number is registered with the shopper's consent. There is a difference between information leaked out and information one entrusts a business operator with based on trust, but seemingly, our commercial credit information is fast becoming part of the public domain and is no longer under our control.

Cases of **victimization by credit card skimming** are being reported with an alarming frequency today. Skimming refers to reading magnetic data on a credit card and copying it to a forged card for illegal use. It is said that data theft tends to occur more frequently when you keep your credit card in a locker at public places like an amusement park, when you hang your coat with your card in one of its pockets on the backrest of a chair at a restaurant, etc., and in other situations where your attention tends to stray from your personal belongings. In an overwhelming majority of cases, because the card itself does not disappear as it would if you were robbed, you do not become aware of having had your card skimmed until you begin to receive statements that do not make sense to you.

Accelerated technological innovation is needed more than ever before, including the introduction of a personal identification environment based on biometric technology, advanced IC chips, etc. After all, self-defense by the individual card user has limitations. Under the existing circumstances, the best we can do by way of self-protection against abuse and fraud is to go back to the very basic principle of card-carrying: **Always keep your credit card next to you.**

KEY POINT

Credit card crimes are growing technically more sophisticated year after year, and people are normally slow in realizing that they may have been victimized.

Recommendations

All credit-card users should:

1. Change their customer ID (secret) number with deliberate frequency (avoiding combinations that may give away their identity);
2. Make routine entries in bank book periodically. (this will help you notice any suspicious transactions early, minimizing any loss);
3. Not carry their credit cards when it is not necessary to do so.

How to Protect Yourself Against Credit Cards Skimming (2)

Cases of forgery and illegal use of credit cards by skimming are rapidly increasing. Such a situation notwithstanding, banks appear to be slow in redressing, or doing anything about the damages sustained by their victimized customers.

Along with damage to credit cards, **damage to bank cash cards** also poses a serious problem. In both cases, magnetic data is read off the card by a method known as "skimming" for illegal use of the stolen data.

Trends in Credit Card Crime Recognition and Indictment Situation reports that, for 2000, there were 3,622 cases of recognized credit card skimming and 2,997 cases of recognized cash card skimming, showing that there were fewer cases involving cash cards than those involving credit cards. This trend continued unchanged from 1998 through 2000. But cash card damages account for larger amounts of money. With credit cards, there is the fear of not realizing until much later that one has been robbed, but because an upper limit is set on the amount that can be debited, no purchase can be made of an extremely expensive item, and this serves as a protection against big losses. But, using a forged cash card, the thief can directly withdraw cash from the victim's bank deposit account. There are uncountable reports of victims complaining, "Without being aware of it, I've had several millions of yen withdrawn from my account in tens of separate transactions."

The basic issue boils down to concerns about compensation for actual monetary losses sustained. There was a preceding period during which credit card fraud cast a large shadow over society as a major social issue, but today credit card issuer companies are insured by credit card insurance policy, and a system is in place to protect card users in the event of any credit card fraud. But banks have not been positively forthcoming in dealing with the cash card compensation issue.

The **credit card regulations currently in effect** (as of 20 July 2005) provide that "to the extent that the customer cannot be proven faultless, the bank shall be exempted of responsibility," which, in fact, absolve the bank of guilt. This is a fundamentally misconceived premise. While it is a fact that part of the funds which the bank uses for investment and other credit-creating purposes has been withdrawn, the bank's financial resources are money "on loan" from its depositors. Protection of the customer (the depositor) is not seen as the bank's responsibility.

Today banks are more open to paying out compensation provided that they are unable to demonstrate that the damage incurred was the result of the depositor's error. But need remains for a change in thinking. Namely, the risk-ridden environment must be redefined as a fulcrum of pro-active business strategizing. If, as credit card companies have done, banks participate in an insurance system exclusively for banks, and/or establish a mutual-benefit system to guard against losses through the formation of an inter-bank mutual-help organization, that will help a positive credit-fomenting environment to develop and provide banks, now reeling from the **lifting of the payoffs ban** (after April 2005), with opportunities for new client acquisition.

KEY POINT

When cash card forgery and fraud by skimming is perpetrated, the case should be regarded as a technical failure on the part of the

bank unless it is demonstrably clear that the card user was at fault. Instead of questioning who should be responsible for the loss, the parties concerned should identify and adopt a measure that will make it possible to redefine the risk-ridden environment as a fulcrum of pro-active business strategizing.

Recommendations

The customer should:

1. Change their customer ID (secret) number with deliberate frequency (avoiding combinations that may give away their identity);
2. Make routine entries in their bank book periodically. (That will help them to notice any suspicious transactions early, minimizing any loss.)

The bank should:

1. Introduce a card insurance system as credit card companies have done;
2. Establish a mutual-benefit system to provide compensation for fraud through the creation of an inter-bank mutual-aid organization.

Risk Management for Government and Businesses: Cases 63–101

Why Businesses should not Neglect On-Going Training

If you cannot practice contingency training in a sustained and deliberate manner, your crisis management system will fail you at the moment of truth.

In the aftermath of an earthquake or a typhoon when the memory of the horror and the scale of the damage is still fresh, people would earnestly work out a training plan and proceed to implement it enthusiastically in preparation for the next big event.

As the saying goes, "**Once past the throat, the heat** (of the food) **is forgotten**" (once on shore, we pray no more). In other words, as memory of the disaster recedes, the sense of urgency for training fades. In many cases, if it should happen that the person in charge of the training or implementation is replaced, the programme may become more textbook-bound and less experimental, or held less frequently, depending on the new person in charge.

The same may be said of **emergency-time customer service policy**. At the time of the Great Hanshin-Awaji Earthquake, IBM was able to maintain its customer service through the post-tremor period. It has been said that IBM was positioned to provide such a service because, in preparation for an emergency, it had in place a round-the-clock customer-service-capable team and an auto-call system in order to immediately address any computer abnormalcy. This had been set up during a time of normalcy and the staff had been regularly trained to operate in such an emergency.

Furthermore, it is said that the company's operational setup requires that the forwarding of messages/instructions to be handled with utmost care when there is a change of managers of emergency food supplies and equipment. The system in place is also structured in such a way that the top management can at any time issue instructions directly to the manager on duty.

The Tokyo factory of Asahi Breweries collaboratively participates in fire drills and related activities at the nearest fire station, and reportedly more and more of the brewery employees are acquiring certified fireman qualification.

Positive efforts such as these — not only to hold periodic, thorough training sessions and drills during ordinary times, but also to maintain collaborative ties with the community and holding joint training sessions with outside parties — should never be neglected.

But the most important point in this regard has to do with how to maintain, on a sustained basis, a mental state of preparedness for future emergencies. It goes without saying that, to such an end, top management and others in responsible positions need to remain vigilant and flexible.

KEY POINT

Once past the throat, the heat (of the food) **is forgotten.**

Recommendations

Businesses should:

1. Install a permanent team of customer service personnel available round-the-clock;
2. Install the auto call system;
3. Increase the number of employees with fireman certification.

Case **64**

Why a Physical Distribution System is Necessary

Your contingency plan will not succeed if your post-tremor distribution scheme is not sufficiently well organized.

Once a major earthquake strikes, it is of the utmost urgency to secure food, clothing and shelter for the victims. After securing shelter, unless the weather or climate is exceptionally disruptive, the next problem to take care of is securing food.

To prepare for the likelihood of supplies from supermarkets and convenience stores being cut off, it is necessary, while there is time for it, to put a working **emergency physical distribution system** firmly in place.

In this regard, the responsive action taken by 7-Eleven Japan, the largest convenience store chain in Japan, at the time of the Great Hanshin-Awaji Earthquake was quite extraordinary.

The relief operation delivered food by ship and helicopter to relay depots, and from there destination-specific deliveries were made by motorcycle or even by foot. Use of helicopters in anticipation of land route blockages and a systematic securing of necessary personnel mirrored know-how built up through real-life experience in overcoming transportation challenges during traffic jams.

Emergency transportation was operated from 17 January through 27 with seven helicopters and 150 motorcycles mobilized. Remarkably, from 18 January to 21, 16,000 pieces of rice balls were delivered to Kobe as relief supplies every day, totaling 64,000 pieces for the four-day period. If distributed at the average rate of two pieces per person, the food would have helped more than 30,000 disaster victims (*Nikkei Business Daily*, **30 January 1995**).

Moreover, these rice balls were made at factories in locations as far removed as Hiroshima and Shiga and then shipped to a heliport in Kobe.

But the majority of organizations and business enterprises have no such emergency distribution scheme planned, and we have seen many instances of shortages of food and other supplies in the wake of disasters. In that sense, it is no exaggeration to say that contingency plans without an emergency distribution system is as good as useless.

KEY POINT

A good distribution system secures peace of mind.

Recommendations

A good distribution system should:

1. Provide for food, clothing, shelter and other provisions;
2. Include *Onigiri* (rice balls) a particularly important food item.

How to Compensate for an Incomplete Crisis Management Education

Although the relevance of contingency planning or crisis management is generally recognized, it is not taught as a subject in schools. This does not help to nurture crisis management awareness.

Planning for contingencies and crisis management are discussed in numerous books, some with rather scary titles like *A Major Earthquake Strikes Tokyo* (Megumu Mizoue [ed] Chukei Publishing [1993]).

In spite of the experts declaring the situation to be as serious as they say it is, no textbooks have been dedicated to the topic, nor has a comprehensive curriculum been developed. All that is provided for students is a once-off experience in the form of occasional training using simulation models.

Why is it, one wonders, that the Central Government does not vigorously promote the education and, applied research of crisis management averting an instantaneous loss of many lives to disaster? Aside from several state-run research organizations, why is it that educational institutions and research establishments will not invest in this field more aggressively?

It may well be that curricula are already swamped, with no room for any more new subjects. It is also possible that experts who can produce adequate textbooks have yet to be trained. Also, introducing a new subject haphazardly would only add a new examination subject.

Be that as it may, we can no longer continue to turn a blind eye to planning for contingencies or crisis management as well as relevant research, which are all of vital interest to the State and society.

It is this author's studied opinion that the time has come for educational institutions, as well as research organizations, in both public and private sectors to address this issue earnestly.

KEY POINT

War is not to be forgotten in times of peace.

Recommendations

All organizations should ensure the following:

1. Officers in charge of provisions, equipment and facilities must handle message transfers with surefire accuracy;
2. Periodical training must be conducted with simulated exercises;
3. Joint exercises must be organized with the adjacent community and collaborative ties expanded beyond the organizational bounds;
4. The number of certified fire fighters must be increased;
5. Evacuation drills to the nearest emergency facility must be conducted.

How Effective Life Protection Products Could Be Developed

Your crisis management setup is incomplete without a quick-response post-tremor life protection system and other pertinent measures.

A number of measures can be taken to prevent building collapse and secure the safety of people's lives immediately after an earthquake.

The first to-do item is to relocate as many people as possible into buildings with earthquake-resistant or seismically-isolated structural features. It is imperative for builders to increase the number of such buildings and not build in lots with unstable, subsidence-prone ground or areas with liquefaction-prone characteristics. These considerations will help to protect human lives, but additional **measures of protecting human lives** must be adopted to complete the effort.

Experience from the Great Hanshin-Awaji Earthquake, the Taiwan Earthquake, the Tottori Earthquake and other similar events show that pieces of furniture that are apt to fall, such as wardrobes, shelves, etc., should be fastened to the nearest pillars or sturdy walls. If you are purchasing new bulky furniture, make sure to choose items that come with metal fittings and other fastening devices.

Even with these preparations in place, the ceiling could fall, or the wall to which standing pieces of furniture are fastened could give way. What is one to do then? *Earthquake Disaster Prevention*

Handbook (1995, the Ministry of Finance Printing Office and Ministry of Internal Affairs Fire Service Agency Anti-Earthquake Disaster Measure Implementation Guidance Office) and *Disaster Prevention Manual for Metropolitan Regions* (1995, p. 91; PHP Research Institute) give the following instructions:

> "Cover your head with a *zabuton* (floor cushion), crawl under a desk and hold on to one of its legs. In other situations, especially in the case of high-rise buildings, desks will themselves shake violently, and so, if it is not dangerous to do so, look for a place where you will not be crushed by falling or collapsing objects, and throw your arms tightly around anything that is sturdy and fixed to the building and is a safe distance away from the window."

If there is room for an even more innovative idea, would it not be possible to develop bedroom airbags, an applied use of the automotive airbag? If such airbags could be designed to be fixed to beds, fixed-type wardrobes, etc., they could instantaneously be deployed to counter falling ceilings and tumbling pillars, possibly protecting people from being crushed to death. The spaces created by these deployed airbags could provide exit routes. At the same time, a foldable, portable airbag carried round the clock could turn out to be a life-saver by deploying instantaneously when falling objects and other surprises should suddenly materialize.

Life protection products should be developed immediately and made available as soon as possible to as many people as possible as necessary items of daily use.

KEY POINT

It takes just a little flair in inventiveness or creativity to save lives.

Recommendations

Remember to do the following during an earthquarke:

1. Cover your head with a cushion. If there is a desk, hide under it.
2. Hang on tightly to a structural feature of the building that is safely away from a window.

Case 67

Why the Need to Develop Next-Generation Disaster Prevention Technologies

A contingency plan not based on next-generation technology is short on effectiveness. Crisis management is then more likely to fail.

If the effectiveness of a contingency plan is to be enhanced, unceasing efforts to develop technologies that will consistently focus on surmounting the exigencies of disaster cannot be dispensed with.

For instance, we assume that the flexible-system concept of structural design is a basic requirement for an earthquake-prone environment. If a system is flexible, no mechanical impact will immediately destroy, bend or damage, or tear it apart; and even if its shape undergoes some change, it can be restored to its original form.

This design philosophy is applicable not only to buildings, but also to other structures using flexible building materials such as pipelines, road surfaces, doors and window frames. Condos built with tremor-proof (seismically isolated) rubber pillars made of laminated rubber components are gaining in popularity.

It is conceivable airbags that can be developed to be fastened to beds and pillars (*cf.* Case 66). Airbags are activated when subjected to a powerful impact and it protect people from falling objects and collapsing artifacts, and, at the same time, create exit spaces.

If such airbags can be designed to be portable, they may well improve the probability of saving lives in critical moments and situations.

It is also important, in the development of next-generation disaster prevention technologies, to accord due attention to the possibility of adapting military technology for civilian applications.

For example, we can make use of infra-red-tracking fire-extinguishing missiles in combination with infra-red cameras and infra-red sensors equipped with built-in missile, to automatically direct flying fire extinguishers at given fire sites. Moreover, if they could be made to explode at a low mid-air altitude above the fire site, they could be an even more effective means of fire fighting with potential for wider use than if they were simply aimed directly at the fire.

It is also important to develop improved versions of the provisions and **supplies kits** developed and used by the armies of other countries as well as by Japan's Self-Defense Forces.

Only by persevering with efforts such as those described above can we hope to be able to alleviate damage from any disaster.

KEY POINT

Unceasing effort helps to alleviate damage.

Recommendations

Researchers and inventors should:

1. Attend and take part in disaster prevention events (expos, exhibitions, shows, etc.) in support of efforts to develop new technologies and new products.
2. Develop methods and technologies for alleviating unnecessary casualties and injuries in times of disaster.

Case **68**

How Products Could Be Developed in Support of Disaster Response

A close look is being directed at the likely economic damage that would be incurred, should an earthquake of the direct-hit type occur in the southern Kanto Plain region. It is important to know in advance how people would behave when affected by a disaster.

Convenience stores carry a map entitled *Map to Help You Get Home in Time from an Earthquake Disaster — Metro Tokyo Edition*. In an earthquake public means of transport will come to a standstill, leaving commuters in the cold with no choice but to walk home. The compact *Home-Bound Routing Guide* was prepared for just such a purpose.

It included detailed homeward path-finding help starting from the central district of Tokyo and emanating in different directions, one bound for southern Saitama Prefecture, others for northeastern Kanagawa Prefecture, southwestern Ibaraki Prefecture, western Chiba Prefecture, etc. What made the pocket-size *vade mecum* particularly useful is that the recommended homeward routes to the various regions were each accompanied by detailed, specific information such as **Wide-Area Evacuee Accommodation Facility**, **Useful Comments for Home-Bound Wayfarers** (about main danger zones/ stretches along the route, [rest area] benches, etc.), **Public Toilets**,

Water Foundation (availability of drinking water along the route), **Home-Bound Wayfarer Assistance Station** (Tokyo Municipality-designated home-bound wayfarer assistance stations), etc.

Just to give an example, the environs of the Hongo, Bunkyo-ku, Tokyo area, where the author resides, are served by Itabashi-bound Hakusan-dori Street, the recommended homeward route, along which there are shown to be a number of convenience stores. Also identifiable are filling stations which will presumably be equipped to provide support and assistance in an earthquake disaster as are the campus of the University of Tokyo and Koishikawa Botanical Garden, which are designated as wide-area evacuee accommodation facilities. The guide is a pocket-size, compact edition of easy-to-use design. Assumptions of severe damage resulting from an earthquake of the direct-hit type at some point in the future in the southern Kanto Plain is public knowledge nowadays, and the guide is probably one indication of how enterprises in the private sector are beginning to show increasingly serious interest in **developing products addressing how one could copy with the aftereffects of a major earthquake**.

There appear to have been publications of the **Hazard Maps** type, prepared and distributed by municipalities in the past, but they appear to have been primarily concerned with predicting the aftermath of a disaster, omitting much detailed discussion in light of the purpose of their publication. Government agencies are well capable of compiling damage predictions on the basis of earthquake disaster assumptions, and it is fair to assume that they have always had a greater understanding than private-sector enterprises of commuters being stranded on their way back home in given areas under their respective jurisdictions. Government agencies should certainly be able to come up with a clearer picture of what type of assistance would be most useful for stranded home-bound commuters and what kinds of support would be necessary.

Reportedly, it is said that municipalities "cannot even afford to allocate financial resources for creating hazard maps." Collaborative linkage between municipalities and private-sector enterprises is necessary. Municipalities could publish earthquake-disaster-generated damage predictions, predictions of situations in which home-bound commuters are stranded, and the necessary support for them. Private-sector enterprises, for their part, based on disclosed disaster-related information, could develop products and provide pertinent services.

KEY POINT

For purposes of working out anti-earthquake disaster measures, a collaborative effort between government agencies concerned and private-sector enterprises it is more likely to had highly significant results.

Recommendations

1. Municipalities should proactively make their disaster predictions public.
2. Based on the disaster-related information disclosed by municipalities, private corporations should engage in developing products that will help victims by providing appropriate services.

Case 69

What Criteria to Use in Assessing a Crisis

Without an adequate understanding of four criteria in handling a crisis, your crisis management will be doomed to fail.

When you are dealing with a crisis, every second counts. It is also required that you have a sufficient understanding of the following four criteria:

First: Judge the **gravity of the crisis**. A misstep committed here will cause a delay in the initial response, which will result in a further aggravation of the crisis. There was much criticism of the initial judgment made by the Government and local municipalities on the Great Hanshin-Awaji Earthquake.

Second: Judge whether the crisis appears **likely to be protracted** and **aggravated**. In a major earthquake in which lifeline disruptions occur, it is normal for the restoration of such damage to take time. To make matters worse, aftershocks may demolish buildings which have somehow managed to stay standing, adding to the outbreak of additional conflagrations, contributing to a further deepening of the crisis.

Third: Judge **what impact the crisis is likely to bring on you and your organization**. If your company building is destroyed or your machinery and equipment are damaged in a major earthquake, a pro-active judgment will be required as to how much time and cost will be incurred to restore the earlier level of business activity and how the business activity is to be maintained in the meantime. If your crisis management manual contains clear instructions regarding an alternative business setup, you have the blessings of forethought.

Fourth: Judge whether there is a **way open for survival** beyond the crisis.

In the United States, Manville Corporation went bankrupt under the unbearable burden of thousands of lawsuits brought against it for the health damage its asbestos-containing building materials had caused. On the other hand, when Apollo 13 was on its way back to the earth, the control center on the earth side and the Apollo crew kept in constant touch for the minutest consultations and, through the productive meeting of minds, successfully dealt with successive crises to make the crew's safe return home possible.

Now that the Product Liability Act is in effect, we may start seeing PL-bankrupted companies in Japan, too. For hints on how to overcome hurdles thrown in your way, it will be important to envision all sorts of conceivable scenarios, study various real cases that happened in America, and assiduously see what lessons can be learned from them.

KEY POINT

Never giving up opens the way to the conquest of crises.

Recommendations

To hone our judgment skills, we must:

1. Acquire value judgments and quick-responding action skills in different types of crisis.
2. Repeatedly perform simulated actions and experiments.

Case 70

What are the Crisis Management Efforts Directed At?

From the standpoint of the residents, it stands to reason that the greater the efforts poured into crisis management and disaster prevention, the greater the expectations for the yield. But if paying attention is neglected, crisis management efforts could end up misdirected.

According to a survey conducted by the daily newspaper *Asahi Shimbun* (24 August 1995) on the subject of "Regional Disaster Prevention Plan," 42 prefectures (with the exclusion of Kanagawa, Aichi, Shizuoka, Tottori and Kochi from a total of 47 Japanese prefectures) and 11 *seirei* cities* (with the exclusion of Yokohama-city from a total of 12 Japanese *seirei* cities), (the excluded regions "have no intention of changing [the existing plan]"), were in the midst of revamping the existing configuration of damage assumption in the aftermath of the Great Hanshin-Awaji Earthquake.

The main points of the revised version concern the seismic magnitude assumption to be reset to 7; and the assumption of the earthquake's epicenter being at the Prefectural Complex.

With the assumed conditions now set more severely than before, there has arisen a need to correctly inform the area residents

---

* Government-Ordinance-designated cities with a population of more than 500,000.

specifically in what way the new disaster-prevention preparation will differ from the old one. The area residents, for their part, will have to begin to **strengthen the communication link** with their Prefectural head.

From September 1995, the Metropolitan Government of Tokyo began to invite residents to fax in proposals concerning disaster prevention. The October Town Hall Meeting with the Governor was dedicated to the topic of disaster prevention.

Moreover, it will also become necessary to hold a periodic **Residents' Congress** to define clearly the roles to be played by the State, local administrative bodies (municipalities, etc.) and area residents toward **regional disaster prevention reinforcement**.

Unless communication routes such as these are effectively operational, it will be difficult to implement disaster prevention and crisis management plans satisfactorily. The most important thing will be to verify who is able to implement recommended proposals, and when and to what extent each person can do so.

KEY POINT

To know which roles could more effectively apply recommended crisis management proposals in previous disaster, and when and to what extent each person could do so, is far more important than to keep making one new proposal after another.

Recommendations

1. Regional authorities should keep residents up to date in a timely manner on newly revised items of the crisis management plan.
2. The authorities should develop more video presentations to help as many area residents as possible have access to pertinent information.
3. When attending a meeting with the crisis management overseer, residents should take accurate notes of the action plans alongside their given deadlines.

Case **71**

How to Maintain Communication Between Operations Staff, Residents and Specialists

_____

If your disaster prevention plan for earthquakes, tsunamis, typhoons, etc., is to be as close to perfect as possible, ongoing communication is necessary between the person assigned to area disaster prevention, area residents and specialists with area disaster prevention know-how. However, there are very few prefectures in the country that practice this.

The Great Hanshin-Awaji Earthquake not only destroyed buildings housing government offices, but also made it impossible for more than half the local government employees to report to work. When an earthquake with a magnitude of 7 or more strikes, it is not always the case that the area disaster prevention plan and crisis management system, even if they are in good working order, will function as they were designed to.

If such a situation occurs, instead of waiting for the area disaster prevention operations head to make a judgment, it becomes necessary for the area residents to operate from their own **appropriate, independent judgments**.

To such an end, it becomes important for each and every area resident to make constant efforts to learn disaster prevention know-how from disaster prevention specialists, seek explanations about emergency do's and don't's from the disaster prevention officer, and

hold regular team meetings and discussions for mock emergency exercises.

For example, one could assume a disaster-stricken situation in which a supply storage created at a local school becomes inaccessible because the employee of the local government or the school employee charged with the management of the storage had been affected by the disaster. One solution would be for several area officers to each keep a duplicate of the storage key.

Furthermore, there would be need for area resident meetings to be organized where consulting organizations such as Kokusai Kogyo, Oyo Corporation and Mitsubishi Research Institute, each assigned with regional disaster prevention development projects, could be asked to present reports on geological surveys covering the quality of the soil, of given areas, discuss the possibility of earthquakes, explain how the effects of an earthquake could spread, were one to occur, etc. At such meetings, it would be paramount not only to project damage assumptions, but also to study in real-life terms what types of emergency relief, order restoration and normalcy recovery measures would be provided by the government, what would be feasible and what not, etc.

KEY POINT

For everyone in the community to be prepared for emergency, there must be regular communication between residents, consultant groups, crisis specialists and other parties concerned in normal times.

Recommendations

1. Residents should periodically seek disaster prevention know-how from disaster prevention specialists.
2. They should also be familiar with what support the government would provide in the way of emergency measures as well as restoration and recovery operations when a disaster strikes.
3. The government should have a thoughtfully prepared quick-response setup in place to support the evacuation of parties requiring assistance during a disaster.

Case 72

Why the Atomic Industry Must Maintain Ongoing Dialog With Its Community

Specialized industries such as the atomic industry, not being widely understood, have the potential to arouse fear in people. Going beyond ordinary safety management, those concerned must search for a way to win the trust of the population and assure their peace of mind.

The 1999 **marine accident at the Ibaraki Prefectural Tokai Village JCO (Japan Nuclear Fuel Conversion Co.)** site sent a major shockwave throughout Japanese society, and the entire nation's concerns were focused on it as a result of extensive media coverage. Undisciplined, illegal handling of a uranium nitrate solution using buckets was ultimately determined to have been the cause for this accident in which a **radioactive gas** with a concentration exceeding a set level had leaked to expose two on-site workers to deadly doses of radioactivity. The compensation for economic loss, including damages to many unsettled cases, has been reported to amount to several tens of billions of yen. This was an accident that brought to the fore much to ponder about Japan's nuclear policy.

Historically, the operation of atomic facilities is very tightly controlled in such areas as safety management and compliance, with applicable restrictions and operating conditions provided for in the

Law for the Regulation of Nuclear Source Materials, Nuclear Fuel Materials and Reactors and the Electric Power Industry Law stipulated by the Atomic Energy Basic Law. Punitive measures are defined for acts of non-compliance on the part of nuclear reactor operators, and they have been made increasingly onerous over time. But, in reality, a corporate culture favoring greater productivity and deemphasizing disaster prevention is pervasive industry-wide, resulting in the condoning of dangerous behaviors. Illegal practices have been perpetrated for many years.

What are others in the same line of business to learn from this incident? Double-checking the existing organizational management setup based on **compliance with relevant laws and regulations** is one, however, what is perhaps even more important is to win the trust and ensure the peace of mind in which the company operates. In this connection, the following two points are pertinent:

1. Let people know of the risk management process which your company practices (your company's constant self-help effort) with a thoroughness that surpasses set standards.
2. Adhere to an attitude which dictates that you clarify for people any point about your business that strikes them as vague and obscure.

For the first point, creation and operation of a management objective system in risk management, based on certain guidelines such as JISQ2001 (Guideline for the Building of a Risk Management System), could prove useful as a frame of reference. It has no legally binding power, but it would underscore the company's commitment to its self-help effort.

The second point is a proposal which typifies what has been verified in social psychology. Generally speaking, specialists and non-specialists use different yardsticks in their perception of danger. It is said that specialists perceive a given danger in a manner that is consistent with what objective data indicates, while non-specialists' perception is influenced by data with emotive effects such as fear.

The following two points, then, sum up the corporate posture companies in this field should uphold consistently:

1. Maintain ongoing dialog with the community, centering on area residents.
2. Continually provide objective data on business-related facts; pro-actively respond to requests for disclosure to resolve issues arising from lack of clarity.

There is room for patient, constant dialog.

KEY POINT

The nuclear industry constitutes a special-category manufacturing sector. Inspite of the technological and economical benefits it brings to the community the latter is ambivalent about its existence. The importance of an exact and comprehensive safety management within the organization cannot be overemphasized, nor can constant communication with area residents as well as publicity to address the significance of the industry's existence.

Recommendations

The nuclear industry must:

1. Constantly disseminate information about their corporate endeavors in compliance with safety management requirements;
2. Keep explaining whatever is perceived as lacking in clarity about their business activity.

How the Multi-Faceted Check
System Works

The effectiveness of CP is closely related to the check system. Without sufficient checks, crisis management is bound to fail.

The "**Check system**" refers to the system of periodic diagnosis, examination and auditing that concerns the mental and bodily health of the state and society in a broader context, and organizations and individuals in a narrower context.

In the history of society, we come across uncountable cases in which success turned into failure, victory into defeat and healthy people fell ill precisely because no check system was in place and fully functioning.

In the corporate context, a check system may work in the form of periodic reviews by executives, advisers or advisory groups; auditing of external board members, society, corporate business, accounting and environment; checking on the legal, social and ethical aspects; monitoring of various types; corporate governance and internal governance one hears about with increasing frequency these days; and checking as a function of the conscience and circumspection of individuals concerned.

These check functions usually incorporate a **check on the CP system**. But it is a fact that, overburdened by day-to-day work, work pertaining to emergency measures, etc., one tends to keep putting the check on "what to do in the unlikely event of" scenarios on the back burner.

It is therefore necessary, regardless of its potential impact or scope, for the system to include and periodically perform both a check on the **regular day-to-day work** and **the normal state of things** and a check on any **emergency response-related work** and any **abnormal state of things**.

As long as the different check systems are correctly set up and are functioning normally, it should be possible to minimize any damage if an emergency were to occur. But once the system ceases to function normally, not only will the damage not be minimized, but there will be a chain reaction of casualties, much like what happened when financial institutions collapsed one after another some time ago. **Checking your check system** will be the first step in reducing or eliminating the failure of your CP.

KEY POINT

Examination is the first step of prevention.

Recommendations

1. A company's top executives and board must conduct periodical reviews of the business.
2. It must be prepared to receive advice from external board members.
3. It must install as wide a variety of monitors as warranted.

How Indirect Damages May Far Surpass Your Assumptions

For crisis management budget appropriation purposes, it is a fairly common practice to calculate the total amount on the basis of a direct damage estimation and an indirect damage estimation. But if the latter is disproportionately underestimated as compared to the former, the budget formulation will fail.

In calculating a **crisis management budget** for earthquake damage, one would think of tackling obvious items first. Normally one starts with directly calculable damaged assets, for example figuring out the extent of the loss due to the collapse of the head office building, the factory structure, and other items. while taking into account the applicable seismic magnitude. Estimations of this type are not so difficult to the extent that items can be cumulatively added up, for example starting from big-ticket assets such as key experiment stations and supercomputers and going down to less expensive items such as personal computers (or a LAN system).

But when it comes to **indirect damage estimations**, the calculations involved are not so simple. Earthquakes and a few other natural disasters can be written off as regrettable acts of heaven, but in the case of man-made disasters, for example, should bad products be circulated in the market, there are certain to surface unforeseen expenses one after another, such as measures to combat loss of trust in the company, compensation for lost earning opportunity, relocation cost, litigation cost, just to name a few. One will, if belatedly, be made aware of what incredible savings a preventive measure would have offered.

We might learn a lesson or two from the incident of 26 February 1993 in New York, in which the underground level of the World Trade Center building was attacked with massive explosive devices. Alongside the explosion of the Alfred P. Murrah Federal Building in Oklahoma City in 1995, this incident was an act of terrorists that killed and injured many innocent citizens.

After the incident, issues of compensation for lost days of work for victims and other parties concerned, relocation cost, etc. were quickly raised, and the costs added up during the first three days amounted to some $300 million. Repair costs for destroyed portions of the building and equipment were estimated at approximately $60 million. Thus, the costs of indirect damage worked out to almost 500 percent of the costs of direct damage.

Thus, indirect damage costs, in many cases, may far surpass assumptions because they tend to have farther-reaching **ripple effects**.

KEY POINT

In the framework of the total damage estimate, pay more attention to indirect damage estimation than to direct damage estimation.

Recommendations

1. Depending on the type and scope of a given disaster, one should calculate not only the direct damage estimate, but also the indirect damage estimate.
2. When the forecasting is done, one should also calculate the cost of preventive measures for comparative study.

How Management Can Respond Swiftly — the Feed-forward Mode (1)

Action taken by management during an earthquake must in all cases be in the "feed-forward" mode that consciously takes into account what lies ahead. (1)

When a major earthquake strikes without warning, it is impossible to know what is happening on the ground.

When nothing is known about the situation, how does one go about protecting the lives and safety of the victims, pre-emptively figuring out what may follow next; and how early can one distribute emergency supplies of water and food to the victims? It is in such situations that the competence and managerial skills of government and corporate leaders are put to the test.

On 17 January 1995, when the Great Hanshin-Awaji Earthquake occurred, Jun Nakauchi, vice-president of Daiei at the time, arrived at company's head office in Hamamatsu-cho, Tokyo, as officially announced, at 6:20 a.m., within one hour of the tremor. Kazuo Kawa, the then managing director, also arrived about the same time. Several staff members, already on hand, were in the middle of securing contact with numerous stores.

The helicopter carrying managing director Kawa, assigned to head the disaster-site-bound team, was issued a permit at 1:45 p.m.

that afternoon to land on Port Island, a man-made island off Kobe, which had virtually been turned into a mud pool. The helicopter arrived at Harborland at 3 p.m., flying over the 100-meter high Kobe Ohashi Bridge with one-meter wide gash along the center divider and the slab joints unhooked visible from the air. As expected, the telephone lines were severely jammed up, and no connection was possible.

In anticipation of such a contingency, the people at headquarters had rented a **mobile satellite communication set**. At 6 p.m., an INMARSAT (International Maritime Satellite) unit, a satellite communication setup originally used for navigation, was delivered, making exchanges of detailed communication possible between Harborland and headquarters.

Remarkably, before the 10-member team headed by managing director Kawa split into two groups and boarded two helicopters, rice balls and lunch boxes for 1,000 persons had been stowed in the cargo bays of the aircraft. This is one good example of how "what best can be done at the given moment" was executed in an exemplary "**feed-forward**" way.

KEY POINT

A disaster is the ultimate test of the stuff a man is made of.

Recommendations

1. Businesses should keep a satellite communication unit in place, or maintain a working arrangement to rent one at any time.
2. The government should build more heliports.

How Management Can Respond Swiftly — the Feed-forward Mode (2)

Action taken by the management during an earthquake must in all cases be in the "feed-forward" mode that consciously takes into account what lies ahead. (2)

At the time of the Great Hanshin-Awaji Earthquake, there were more than a few corporate management teams who took pro-active action from their reading of what lay ahead.

Daiei, among others, executed in quick succession a series of **"feed-forward" based measures** starting at an early stage in the post-tremor timeline (*cf.* Case 75).

By 8:45 p.m., 17 January, it had arranged emergency food supply which was transported by **helicopter** and, additionally, dispatched a ferry from the Port of Fukuoka. The ferry was bound for the port at Izumi-Otsu, Osaka, not the Port of Kobe; the operations team had obtained information that the damage sustained by the facilities at the Port of Kobe would be too great to allow the ferry's access.

The ferry carried, among other things, portable heaters, food (rice balls, etc.), two tank lorries loaded with drinking water, and other items.

The deployment of these tank lorries was decided at the company's Tokyo headquarters at 8 a.m. by Managing Director Kawa in connection with another decision to ship goods. Mr. Kawa decided to ship free drinking water when nothing specific was as yet known about any damage to the local **lifeline** system.

Action did not end there. Taking into account the possibility that boats' access to the port's quay might not be possible, the operations team had instructed one of the lorries to head for Kobe by land.

The weather bulletin announced heavy rainfall for 21 January. Taking a forward read on the needs of the adversity-stricken, Daiei, working through its available local outlets, released from its Kobe distribution warehouse 20,000 umbrellas, 12,000 foldable lightweight raincoats, 10,000 regular raincoats, rainwear for 15,000 persons, 6,000 vinyl raincoats, and 20,000 rain-proof sheets for those in need.

KEY POINT

Disaster prevention and crisis management must be designed and practiced in the "feed-forward" (preventive and temporally pre-emptive) mode.

Recommendations

1. A setup must be in place that enables, in time of a disaster, the air transport of emergency foodstuffs by helicopter.
2. At the same time, maritime transport must also be available to cover any gap in air transport.

Case 77

How to Predict Disasters

In the management of crises generated by an earthquake and other events, the decision-maker's courageous action is absolutely indispensable. Without it, the loss of many lives will follow.

There are reports that certain animals and plants seem to have the ability to sense the imminence of abnormal phenomena: more than one month ahead of the event in the case of insects, about a week before with fishes and silkworms, and one day before with cows, horses, tortoises, dolphins, etc.

Silkworms, it is said, normally move about in a totally disorganized fashion, but four or five days before a tremor they would begin to form organized columns all heading in the same direction. The day before the Great Hanshin-Awaji Earthquake, dolphins in a local aquarium were seen to be acting unusually, jumping out of the water spontaneously and disobeying their handlers' instructions as they swam about frantically, according to the employees of Suma Aqualife Park in Kobe.

Silk-trees and poplars also seem to show subtle changes. There are research papers describing how some plants detect, and react to, changes in ultra-low underground electric currents occurring before an earthquake. This could be one explanation for this plant behavior.

The 12 March 1995 issue of *Yomiuri Weekly* carried an article by Professor Kiyoshi Wadatsumi of Osaka City University, which summed up as many as 850 premonitory signs of what was to be the Great Hanshin-Awaji Earthquake. Seeing that 1,519 similar premonitory phenomena were being discussed in other weekly magazines as well, one wonders if man might not be the only species lacking in the **ability to foretell disasters**.

In connection with the earthquake that hit western Greece in March 1993, Professor Ballotsos of the University of Athens had detected an abnormalcy in the underground electric current before the disaster and alerted the authorities to the possibility of an imminent earthquake. There were pros and cons regarding whether the citizenry should be warned, but the Mayor of Athens took the courageous step of making what he knew public. When the earthquake came, it demolished some 4,000 homes, but there was no loss of life. Would Japanese politicians have taken similar action?

KEY POINT

At the highest step of courage is the audacity to stand up to danger. (Vauvenargues, "Réflexions et Maximes")

Recommendations

1. The authorities should devise experiments that tap the abilities of animals and plants in forecasting earthquakes.
2. They should also mobilize in learning all realms of knowledge to forecast disaster.

How to Establish a Quick Response Setup

In responding to major earthquakes and other disasters, what we need is a feed-forward type of counter measure. But crisis management will be stymied unless the swift response can flexibly adapt in real time to the changing needs of the victims.

Companies may have in place measures of the "feed-forward" type, discussed elsewhere, but in the meantime the needs of victims on the ground are changing dramatically every minute. It is paramount to have in readiness a **real-time system of quick response to victims' needs**.

For instance, immediately following the outbreak of the Great Hanshin-Awaji Earthquake, **flashlights**, **batteries** and **work gloves** (army gloves used by workers to protect themselves from injuries at accident sites) became instant hot commodities at Lawson convenience stores.

Next on the best-seller list came mineral water and ready-to-eat items such as bread, rice balls and canned food, followed by cup noodles, and beverages. When the situation settled down somewhat, undergarments and dry shampoos began to move.

By day four, more and more people had begun to ask for magazines, game cards and toys, and there were signs indicating that, even in the lives of evacuees, efforts were being made to restore a normal routine. (See *TALISMAN* 1995 Vol. 20, p. 7; Tokio Marine & Nichido Risk Consulting.)

The Lawson stores astutely noted the shifting trend in demand and held on to their continued efforts to keep their store fronts adequately filled with the necessary commodities. To that end, the management had to make the most of their accumulated know-how and continued to keep an eye on when withdraw to previous "hot sellers" and stick upon the latest thing in demand.

The chain pitched tents in a vacant lot on which the Sannomiya Daiei store had once stood to create an outdoor eatery village where disaster victims could drop by for such favorites as *yakitori* (broiled chicken), *oden* (hotch-potch *à la japonaise*), *motsu-nabe* (giblets in a pot), etc. The idea was to offer what little comforting and soothing moments could be put together for the benefit of the traumatized population, hopefully to help restore the nightly animated street scenes and the early return of a resuscitated town.

KEY POINT

In the world you will have tribulation; but be of good cheer, I have overcome the world. (JOHN 16:33)

Recommendations

1. Pro-active businesses grasp the changing demand trend day by day in a disaster-stricken area, and distribute appropriate commodities accordingly.
2. They pay attention not only to basic daily needs (clothing, food and shelter), but also to accommodate wants that can hopefully help to alleviate people's mental anguish and psychological stress.

Case 79

Why a Backup System is Needed

Despite the need to prepare and have in place a CP manual, there is a high probability that readiness for the next unforeseeable event is inadequate precisely because companies, especially the medium to small enterprise, lack the know-how to build their own backup system.

Regardless of business category and business type, one must take steps to make absolutely certain that the same mistake is not repeated by putting together a CP manual too quickly.

Companies affiliated with large corporations in the financial and securities business, which have neither recovered from the Great Hanshin-Awaji Earthquake nor the bursting of the bubble economy, have to some extent put a working backup system in place. But it is said that most of the medium to smaller securities companies simply do not have the constitutional power to set up a desirable CP on their own and build a backup system. As things stand today, it is not possible to create and maintain a setup under which customer data can be securely protected in the event of an earthquake with a seismic magnitude of under 7, let alone higher. A customer contact network can be activated even in an emergency, such that proceeds from the sale of shares can be delivered; and, should a shares deposit receipt be lost in a fire, conversion to money can be made based on a backup copy of it.

If this problem is to be resolved at an early stage, it would be necessary to set up a subsystem or a backup system (or a plurality of such systems) outside of the Metropolitan Region such that the risk could be dispersed.

Larger and older securities firms are envisioning shared use of such systems. This should be all the more applicable to medium and smaller securities companies which cannot afford to bypass the need to design and build a comparable shared use system.

This issue concerns not only the financial and securities industries, but also other industries equally. There cannot be an industry that can with confidence claim that it is impervious to the ripple effects of a major seismic event.

KEY POINT

Only when there is a joint effort is it possible to build a backup system.

Recommendations

1. Even if the securities company finds it difficult to build a backup system by itself, it should not abandon the idea.
2. Working jointly with several other companies, it should build an auxiliary system or replacement system as quickly as possible.

Case 80

How to Counter Weaknesses in Supply Chain Management

A supply chain functions to minimize inventory and is an indispensable tool for activating the flow of production activity. But one needs to be aware that it demonstrates certain weaknesses when facing risks that tend to spread with a ripple effect.

On 22 November 1999 at about 1:40 in the afternoon, an Air Self-Defense Force T33A jet on a training mission crashed into the embankment of River Irumagawa in the city of Sayama in Saitama Prefecture, killing the two high-ranking ASDF crew members aboard. Before hitting the ground, the aircraft cut into high-voltage power transmission lines, causing power outage to some 800,000 homes in parts of Tokyo and Saitama for over three hours.

The damage was to spread further in due course. Its effect on the railway system was far-reaching, affecting five metropolitan systems including the Seibu Ikebukuro Line, and Shinjuku Line, Yurakucho Line of the foundation-operated Eidan Subway System (recently renamed Tokyo Metro), which came to a complete halt for a time. Seven hundred traffic light units supported by the disrupted high-voltage power transmission line straddling the two major urban areas stopped functioning. Scheduled train operations serving home-bound commuters were thrown into chaos. Snarled traffic was seen at intersections up and down the arterial roads of the affected areas. Traders' terminals at some securities companies were disabled. Reportedly, Tokyo Securities Exchange had to stop its interest-rate futures option transactions for about 30 minutes.

The damage extended to hospitals, local government offices, shopping centers and other financial institutions. Irumagawa Hospital in Sayama somehow managed to keep its artificial respiratory machine system going, on which human lives were depending, by using home generators, although its examination equipment could not be operated. This made it impossible to diagnose outpatients, and the surgical interventions scheduled for the afternoon had to be cancelled. Patients using power-driven home-use oxygen inhaler machines had to be rushed to hospitals to use the generator-operated respirators.

At Nerima Ward Office on the Tokyo side and Sayama Municipal Office, not far from the accident site, computers were disabled, resulting in the impossibility of performing such routine tasks as resident identity verification and national health insurance processing. It is said that handwritten certificates had to be issued as a last resort.

At a supermarket opposite the north exit of Sayama Train Station, a pencil-and-scratch-paper quick fix was resorted to by the cashier to process payment from some 20 customers who happened to be shopping at the time; thereafter the store was closed for the rest of the day at a cost of almost a million yen. A flower shop catering to funeral and other ceremonial needs could not receive orders with its telephone and fax out of order.

The Ministry of Posts and Telecommunications (Japan Post) reports that 289 post offices in adjacent wards of Tokyo and western Saitama were affected, with online business disrupted just past 1:40 p.m. Window terminals and ATM's were unusable for more than three hours. The ATMs of branch offices of banks such as Tokyo-Mitsubishi, Fuji (now Mizuho Bank) and Sakura (now Mitsui-Sumitomo Bank), located near the accident site, were unusable for anywhere between several and tens of minutes.

The damage engulfed companies in the private sector as well. Honda Motor's vehicle body and engine factories (Sayama Plant) in

Saitama had their production lines shut down for more than three hours. Apparently the production lines were themselves not directly affected by power failure but had to be stopped because parts delivery by truck was delayed due either to traffic lights and signals on roads not working, or to parts suppliers' production processes having been brought to a standstill.

This vehicle assembly factory was equipped with the latest backup system. But if its secondary and tertiary subcontractors sustained damage, delivery trucks would be late and parts would not be delivered on time, the vehicle factory could not function. One choice would be to over stock the inventory, but this is not a readily acceptable solution.

Yet there is no other way to overcome this inherent weakness in the JIT ("just in time") system as revealed during the Great Hanshin-Awaji Earthquake. At that time, Toyota lived the bitter experience of having the main vehicle body production lines paralyzed for almost four full days.

It must be fully understood that a supply chain basically has a similar built-in weakness. More than ever before, it is necessary to have in place a risk management setup where a constant level of emergency inventory is maintained with the sources of supply diversified such that the flow of production will continue even when unforeseen circumstances materialize.

KEY POINT

To deal with the ripple effect of an event requires the deployment of a counter measure organized in multiplex (spider-web-like) fashion.

Recommendations

1. While normalcy prevails, companies should take time out to make sure that their emergency operating plan is soundly in place to deal with a sudden power outage.
2. They should also repeat as often as is necessary the simulation of a power outage to identify and overcome any weaknesses in the system.

When Reading the Manual Won't Do

Reading the manual is not the same as understanding it.

According to a survey conducted by the Kansai Association of Corporate Executives, of 48 companies which experienced the Great Hanshin-Awaji Earthquake (75 percent of the companies which had been sent a questionnaire), 69 percent of the respondents kept a **crisis management manual** on hand, far outnumbering those that did not, which accounted for 31 percent.

Not a few, however, point out the limitations of a manual. Some express opinions that are tantamount to outright distrust in the usefulness of a manual, maintaining that "there is no scope for a manual except insofar as they address the chain of communication in time of an emergency and the transfer of authority to those in charge on site", or that "even with the help of a manual, the prevailing circumstances (referring to the Great Earthquake) would have made it extremely difficult to take adequate measures".

But, in answer to the question, "Do you think the manual duly fulfilled its function?", 56 percent of the respondents said, "For most practical purposes, yes." This would indicate that a manual is a necessity after all.

Twenty-eight percent of the companies surveyed admitted that they found the manual too simplistically conceived and that things on the ground did not match what had been foreseen in the manual, suggesting that an excellent manual is a tall order. But each company still needs to communicate, protect lives and properties and what it can do to contribute to the community during an emergency.

One can prepare a manual and have it studied, but the point is: How well do the employees who study it grasp the real "teaching" beyond the printed words?

A crisis situation calls for a creative, imaginative interpretation and an intelligent application of the manual, even though its contents may not be explicitly presented as such. If you are delivering merchandise and should unexpectedly find yourself in the middle of a situation where the telephone lines are jammed or disconnected, how do you accomplish your mission? It would be good if you are prepared for such a contingency, but short of that, you will have only yourself to turn to — you with your resourcefulness and quick wits.

KEY POINT

A good understanding of the manual does not always guarantee faultless behavior.

Recommendations

1. All companies must prepare and make available to all concerned a crisis management manual.
2. They should not regard the completed manual as the definitive, unalterable gold standard, but must revise it as often as is necessary to keep it current.

Case **82**

What is the Crux of Crisis Management?

The crux of crisis management or CP boils down to: "Once you give up, the game's over."

Norio Kurisu, who was president of Maruwa Corporation when the Great Hanshin-Awaji Earthquake occurred, expressed his deeply held belief thus, "Yours may be a small company, but this applies to you just as well: **Once you give up, you're at the end of your rope.**" In other words, however dire your crisis situation may be, as long as you do not give up, the way out will eventually open up before you.

When Norio Kurisu arrived at his office in Nagata-ku, Kobe on the morning of 17 January 1995, his office quarter, Factory No. 1 and the warehouse had already been reduced to ashes. Factory No. 2 was completely demolished and the remains of the building were on the brink of being engulfed by approaching flames. All he could do, completely forgetting himself, was to busy himself with fire-fighting.

He was barely able to collect himself at the end of the day when he was surrounded by 14 hard-working employees who in unison kept saying, "We must resume our normal work at any cost!" He built a temporary office shack in a hurry, and, when he contacted his clients three days later, he was immediately swamped with orders.

But the factories which could make the industrial packing and shims (liners), which were part of the company's product lineup, were gone, and so, as a last resort, Kurisu approached a competitor company and was given a helping hand.

Fortune smiled on Kurisu even further. It was with his clients' and others' encouragement that Kurisu applied for and was awarded a grant from Kobe City's Industrial Growth Promotion Section, which enabled him to acquire a 420 sq m lot in an industrial park in Nagata-ku and build on it a temporary factory structure in early March. Kurisu later reported that he could not stop the tears from running down his cheeks.

The experience of Maruwa teaches us that it is not impossible to overcome a crisis even in the most dire of circumstances.

KEY POINT

Giving up marks the beginning of failure.

Recommendations

1. Never give up hope no matter how bad the crisis situation you may find yourself in.
2. In an emergency situation, never dismiss out of hand the importance of trying to win over a rival.

How the *Kamban* (Just In Time: JIT) System can be Tweaked to Support Production

If we were to be obsessed with only the negative evaluation of systems developed in Japan such as the kamban system, in terms of questioning how they would fare in a disaster-stricken situation, we would be losing sight of the crisis management setup as it was originally designed to be.

Immediately after the Great Hanshin-Awaji Earthquake, newspaper and magazine articles began to claim that the disaster revealed the weakness of the **kamban system**. Because of its excessive pursuit of efficiency, it incorporated no contingency plan spelling out what to do if a parts shortage should occur following a major disaster. In fact, Toyota Motor, well-known for its kamban system, had no choice but to stop its entire production line for a period of time after the earthquake.

Tatsuro Toyoda, then president of Toyota Motor, claimed that the occasion made him truly appreciate the merits of the system all the more, and that it was precisely because of the particular production system in place that it was possible to make an early identification of the problem and a quick resolution of it — which in turn facilitated a prompt recovery of the production by working closely with the parts suppliers.

The president was asked on his business trips abroad if, in view of what had happened, he was reconsidering Toyota's existing production setup. He invariably said he had no intention of changing anything. He appeared determined to continue his exertions for inventory reduction and production efficiency improvement.

He said the disaster had helped in identifying early the problem of Toyota purchasing a certain part from a single supplier, which would mean that, if the supplier were to become disabled by some natural disaster, the supplier could not be easily replaced by another supplier who could turn down the small order as unprofitable.

From the standpoint of **risk avoidance**, however, the fact remains that, unless a purchase format were to be embraced that would have a given part supplied by a plurality of suppliers, the factory operation would be interrupted again if another disaster strikes.

Another point that has come to light relates to the necessity of a risk avoidance formula that promotes the streamlining of vehicle types through a design based on parts interchangeability.

Be that as it may, Toyota has declared that it will continue to use its kamban system which will be upgraded and improved on an ongoing basis.

KEY POINT

A defect in a system should be identified through incessant endeavors.

Recommendations

1. Companies must not neglect system evaluation in an emergency.
2. They should also re-examine all production systems from the view point of crisis management.

Case 84

How Managerial Behaviour Matters

A manager in a crisis situation behaves according to one of four principles: defiance, aggressive bravura, quick turn of wits, or feed forward. In crisis management, one cannot minimize the effects of failure without making a judgment call that goes beyond the manager's manual.

Masao Tokutani, former professor of Seikei University, has listed three basic principles of behavior, any one of which a manager in a crisis situation would subscribe to: **defiant reaction**, **aggressive show of bravura**, and **quick turn of wits**. This author wishes to add **feed-forward**, which includes farsightedness, to this list and make it the **four principles of managerial behavior**.

"Defiant reaction" refers to that mental attitude with which the manager, even when he must make **judgments going beyond the crisis management manual**, discards all privileges and limitations conferred on him by position and honor and takes it upon himself with a sink-or-swim determination to look the crisis straight in its face, mobilize all his wits to minimize damage, and deal with the given situation with utmost mental acuity.

Daiei, operator of a nationwide chain of supermarkets and other outlets, lost no time in sending Managing Director Kazuo Kawa as well as Chairman Isao Nakauchi (in office then) to the areas hit by the Great Hanshin-Awaji Earthquake shortly after the event to have them on hand to lead the rescue and order-restoring operations. This made it easy for the company, in a quick, bold move, to temporarily shut down some of its stores. The Chairman, who stopped by at one of the hamburger stores his chain operated, found it closed "because water and gas had stopped flowing." He is reported to have scolded the employee, saying "If you can't flip burgers, why not make rice balls or lunch boxes and sell them?"

"Aggressive show of bravura" is an effective tool to block the relentless exacerbation of a crisis which would continue if those in charge were to flinch or assume a negative stance when facing the issues at hand. If, when a major tremor occurs, one were to give priority to only running away from the building without decoupling the circuit breaker or turning off the main gas stopcock, one would be leaving sources open for a fire.

The third point, "quick turn of wits," refers to the act of thinking fast and doing the right thing instead of unthinkingly resorting to the first thing that comes to mind. A department store fire broke out in Sen-nichi, Osaka in May 1972, killing a total of 118 people. A small group of people who behaved differently from the rest of the crowd were those who had been aware of the **emergency staircase** and who noticed one open emergency exit on that day; they escaped through that exit to safety. It was their quick turn of wits that saved their lives.

KEY POINT

What enhances the chances of survival in a situation where a crisis or disaster poses a grave danger is a quick turn of wits, not an impulse-driven act.

Recommendations

1. When attempting an escape from a danger-ridden building, unless an imminent life-threatening danger is present, make sure to turn off the circuit breaker before leaving the building.
2. Time permitting, turn off the main gas stopcock, too.

How to Tap the Know-How of Security Companies

CP or crisis management plans incorporate the function of collecting information from many sources, both internal and external, when an emergency breaks out. Making light of the information and technology with which security companies are armed, the very tools of their real-time crime prevention and disaster avoidance activities, would only augment the chance of failure.

Security companies such as Sohgo Security Services (ALSOK), Central Security Patrols and Secom (CSP) provide services to protect customers' lives and properties in preparation for any eventuality. Once they fail, they will likely lose the trust of their customers.

To prevent failure, they are therefore equipped with a wealth of instructive know-how and technology that one can learn from in developing CP and crisis management.

The Global Positioning System (GPS), an investment of more than ¥4 billion which ALSOK operates, connects its office computer via a communications satellite to vehicle-mounted terminals which may be located anywhere nationwide to provide two-way information exchange for real-time vehicle positioning. If this system can be operated round the clock, any vehicle caught in an emergency can be issued early-exit or detour instructions.

SECOM CX, a SECOM product introduced in 1989, uses a whole array of remote-controlled, finely tuned services to protect buildings from crimes and disasters to schedule management of climate control, electricity, elevator system and entrances and exits; monitor irregularities to automatic meter readings for electricity, gas and water — all of which make up a major lifeline of tenants.

This shows that, the more sophisticated remote control technology becomes, the greater the possibility that, the scope of damage in an earthquake can be reduced and ensuing disasters prevented. Ever more creative use of remote control technology in emergency situations assumes utmost importance.

KEY POINT

Remote control technology is indispensable for crisis management.

Recommendations

1. Businesses should positively use technology to minimize damage from earthquakes and other disasters.
2. They should also maximize its use for operation and management of vehicles in emergency situations.

Case **86**

How to Protect Your Computers

As the use of personal computer information systems that are typi-cally Internet-based become more and more common, measures of responding to computer-related contingencies assume increasing importance.

Disasters involving information systems are of a wide range and variety, spanning cases brought on by natural disasters such as com-puter destruction and network disruption to criminal activities such as password theft, secret information deciphering and information destruction by means of **computer viruses**.

Ever wider use of the Internet has opened the way for personal computer information systems to be increasingly dispersed and self-contained. It cannot be overemphasized how necessary it has become to design and pro-actively upgrade an effective **computer security** assurance system. It would indeed be disastrous if an infor-mational system were to crash at the most critical moment.

However excellent the computer security measures in place may be, there is no overlooking the fact that hackers and crackers who specialize in keyword deciphering, program alteration and computer virus infiltration are accumulating and refining their experience, know-how and technology.

In 1999 more than 60 viruses were reported, going by names such as "Dark Avenger," "Cascade," "Jerusalem," "Stoned," "Yankee Doodle" and "John." These represent just the tip of the iceberg. One can not be too careful.

In order to block illegal browsing and other activities by a third party via the Internet, a firewall based on packet filtering or application gateware would have to be adopted, as well as security tightened by codifying inter-Internet traffic data.

KEY POINT

Introduce new technologies as are necessary to block outside attempts to steal or destroy information stored on personal computers.

Recommendations

All businesses should:

1. Equip the Intranet with a firewall.
2. Incorporate countermeasures against disasters originating in personal computer communications systems as thoughtfully as possible.
3. Keep to entry/exit procedures for their computer systems and take any other relevant measures in the most thorough manner possible.

Case **87**

How to Guard Against Computer Viruses

Computer viruses are growing increasingly powerful, and the number of victims are on the increase.

According to a report compiled by Information Processing Association (IPA), there were 461 reports of computer virus infection filed with IPA in January 2000, a record monthly figure. Of these, about 90 percent came from companies, far outnumbering reports filed by government agencies.

In 2000, Government agencies and corporations mobilized almost 2 million employees nationwide to beef up their anti-virus setups. Possibly reflecting this tightened stance, only one virus, known as W32/Fix2001, was caught attempting to piggyback on the Y2K scare, and no full-blown damage was reported that was attributed to the so-called "2000 virus," the time-bomb that was expected to emerge.

A microvirus by the name of W97MCHANTAL.A was reported to have been identified overseas: an utterly destructive program that would, if its file were opened in 2000, thoroughly wipe out all the files on the C: drive. There is a looming possibility that variants, or various subspecies, of such viruses will be caught on the prowl.

Trend Micro Incorporated announced in early 2000 that 11 new viruses were found abroad, including a TROJZELO which would overwrite all the files on the C: drive; a VBSLUCKEY2000 which would replace all the files on the root directory with the virus code; and a PESPACES.1633, which, on 1 June every year, would disable system activation by altering the master boot record and which, moreover, is virtually undeletable because it would destroy the original files at the time of the virus infection. As a countermeasure, the company recommends the use of the latest vaccine software, newer than Pattern File version 63.

In view of the rising trends discernible overseas in the number of virus infection cases, PA, for its part, is spreading word about the antivirus software programs it has developed while calling on those concerned to recognize the necessity of collecting relevant information through websites. The current situation, however, is one in which, short of some imagination-defying action, it will continue to be a challenge to take any preventive measure against new viruses.

KEY POINT

Have in place and update your computer virus counter-measures on an ongoing basis. Always attend workshops offering the latest in computer security technology.

Recommendations

All businesses must:

1. Thoroughly educate and train their staff in computer security;
2. Learn from others' experiences of virus infection.

Case 88

Why Risk Financing is an Absolute

CP and crisis management without risk financing (risk-related financial management) is a foregone case of failure.

No **risk management** measure can be said to have been taken by the State, business corporation or household, if they do not have financial management measures soundly in place to alleviate the effects of any loss in the event of a disaster.

Risk financing is normally covered by some form of emergency budget or insurance payment. Thus, depending on the scale of the risk, the budget or insurance payment will naturally vary.

Previously nuclear families which wanted to purchase an earthquake insurance policy would be limited to ¥10 million for the house and ¥5 million for household effects, a total of ¥15 million. It would have been better than no insurance at all, but undeniably there were severely restrictive conditions that made it impossible to quantify reasonable risk insurance for earthquake disasters.

We have today an improved situation in Japan where if we wish to purchase a ¥100 million policy for the house and a ¥20 million policy for household effects, we would be entitled to an **earthquake insurance** policy corresponding to 30–50 percent of the main contract, or a maximum of ¥50 million for the house and ¥10 million for household effects.

Even though there are upper limits to the risk financing available to individual home owners, the important point is that only when financial security is in place to cover the assumed risk can it be said that crisis management measures have been taken.

It goes without saying that the government as well as local public organizations must put together budgets that assume contingencies, but it is equally paramount that individual citizens be ready with pro-active insurance measures to protect their lives and assets.

KEY POINT

Only when preventive measures such as risk insurance have been taken has the first step of crisis management been taken.

Recommendations

1. Earthquake insurance is a must. The policy holder must beware that the contract will assume the form of an attachment to a fire insurance policy.
2. Insurance must be so designed that the protection of life and properties can be realized.

Case 89

How Office Location Affects Crisis Management

Large organizations — government and big business entities in particular — may install a CP or crisis management office, but often, the latter is located such that there is a high possibility that in an emergency they will prove hardly useful at all.

More and more large-scale organizations, both public and private, are housed in high-rise buildings today. In many cases, the chief of the emergency response unit, who functions as the officer responsible for the **Crisis Management Office**, especially in the case of corporations, has his office on the topmost floor, or in its vicinity.

What implications could this have? If the conference room where emergency meetings are held is situated on the second or third floor, it would be quite a challenge to reach the conference room, should a major earthquake occur, as the elevators would be stalled.

Efforts would be made to contact the deputy chief and any or all of the managers concerned via the emergency communications network, but no connections would be possible with the public communications lines disrupted; precious time would be lost without anything meaningful being done.

To make matters worse, should an earthquake of the magnitude of the 1923 Great Kanto Earthquake hit Tokyo in the early morning, most of the emergency response personnel would most certainly not be able to arrive at the head office within two or three hours because the roads would be impassable. Thus, even with an emergency response unit in place, it is highly conceivable that, in an emergency, it will not be able to function according to design.

If the CP office is not to be reduced to a "castle in the air," it is essential that the following three conditions are satisfied: That the office of the chief be relocated to a lower floor; that, a dedicated communication line be kept operational and radio communication be made possible during emergencies; and that a good number of the emergency response personnel reside within walking distance of the head office.

KEY POINT

The crisis management executive organ should not be allowed to be reduced to a castle in the air.

Recommendations

1. The office of the officer responsible for the Crisis Management Office should be situated near the Emergency Control Center.
2. In readiness for an emergency, communications on a dedicated line or by radio must be operational at all times.
3. At least half the emergency response unit should reside within walking distance of the head office.

Case 90

How to Set the Optimum Security Level of Information Systems

As company information systems make progress by leaps and bounds, a systematic management of security strategies is assuming increasing importance today. It is no longer the case that companies adopting measures exclusively for their own loss avoidance are not contributing to the ultimate solution of their problems.

In leapfrog fashion, the evolution of information systems is making for ever greater convenience in the conduct of corporate business. But at the same time, increasingly serious damage has been inflicted by such intrusions as the theft of personal information and secret information, network invasion by outside parties, and information alteration or destruction. To counter this trend, it has for some years now been considered a priority for companies to have systematically structured **information security defense measures** in place. System Research Center Director Zenji Katagata observes that "information security management is as much a company's own self-defense measure as it is a measure for protecting its social trustworthiness." He lists the following five points as essential: (1) Invest in and set up an information security system, (2) maintain an accurate record of information assets, (3) practice risk management, (4) comply with the laws, and (5) be response-ready for a security audit on an ongoing basis.

Companies must exercise caution in setting the **security level** when handling their information systems. If the level is set too low, leaks of personal and management information will occur, opening the door to attacks from the outside. If, on the other hand, the level setting is too high, convenience for the user will suffer, or losses may be incurred. The server on the recipient side will inadvertently reject information from the outside.

The author once had to deal with a case in which an attached e-mail file was rejected because the recipient company's information security policy was set too high, resulting in a virus attack being allowed. Settling the ensuing confusion took up a lot of time from both parties. The company incurred significant loss in terms of opportunity cost.

The following points may be useful in deciding on the optimum security level setting:

1. Analyze the real-life (or, if possible, even the potential) threat to the operation of the company's information system.
2. Calculate the damage it would amount to.
3. To identify the level that meets the given security criterion, determine the cost that can be invested.

For purposes of maintaining the corporate business model, one working criterion for the security level setting may be one that meets the standard of building trust and providing peace of mind for corporate clients as well as not exceeding investment resources. A company whose information security is valid by criteria set by a third-party organization will stand in good stead in competing against other players in the same line of business. The ISMS (Information Security Management System) Promotion Office of the Japan Information Processing Development Corporation (http://www.jipdec.jp/) organizes ISMS workshops and symposia to encourage ISMS compliance evaluation by a third-party certifying organization. Attendance may provide useful leads.

KEY POINT

A company's information security measures must be trustworthy both internally and externally. Identifying the appropriate information security standard helps to reinforce the company's competitiveness and pro-active corporate strategizing.

Recommendations

All companies must:

1. Introduce the "ISMS Compliance Evaluation" system;
2. Double-check on the existing information system not only from the technical standpoint, but also in terms of how the organization is using it in its operations;
3. Taking into account the cost-benefit, evaluate a response setup that should kick in when a new risk factor has been discovered in the information system.

What Lessons were Learned from the Fukuchiyama Line Train Derailment?

Railway companies offer area residents "people mover" services, but more importantly they are vested with a social responsibility as lifeline service organizations to provide safety and peace of mind.

In April 2005, the worst **train derailment** ever in the history of Japan Railways occurred in which 107 people were killed and 461 injured (latest figures as of 8 May 2005), when a train derailed on the Western Japan Fukuchiyama Line (between Tsukaguchi Station and Nirasaki Station), within the city limits of Amagasaki, Hyogo Prefecture.

The five foremost coaches derailed, of which the first two crashed into a condo complex and, according to one report, were virtually demolished beyond recognition. Investigations were conducted by the Hyogo Prefectural Police and the Aircraft and Railway Accidents Investigation Commission of the Ministry of Land, Infrastructure, Transport and Tourism. While the definitive cause for the accident still remains to be identified, a number of theories and issues have been advanced, including: stones were intentionally placed on the rails, the train was speeding, something caused the coaches to be lifted off the tracks, insufficient training of operators and "re-education" of operators with a record of accidents, a punitive work environment.

As is the case with the March 2000 **Subway Hibiya Line Derailment**, the task of identifying the fundamental cause is fraught with difficulties. It is thought that a compound set of causes may well have been involved. It is hoped that the investigation by the Ministry of Land, Infrastructure, Transport and Tourism will lead to an early identification of the cause of the accident and an implementation in time of measures to prevent a recurrence. This should center on the redesigning of the legal framework required for service operation. "Take care of the safety, and peace of mind will follow" was an idea propagated by media programs, and it certainly resonates at a deep level.

It is important for railway companies, and its customers, to renew the recognition of the railway service as one of the lifelines of daily life. It is the recognition that, alongside other services, the railway service is an **enterprise vested with a vital and hefty social responsibility**. The railway service is an essential service as such public utilities as roads, water service, power supply and telecommunications. The **Lifeline industry** is accorded a higher degree of priority in the daily lives of citizens than other service industries, and is expected to provide services with safety and peace of mind factored in.

JR Fukuchiyama Line was in a route conflict with Hankyu Electric Railways Takarazuka Line. At the time of the accident, Fukuchiyama Line was operating an overcrowded train schedule in order to differentiate its service from its competitor's, increasing the number of train operations and stations where rapid trains would stop (under the 2003 revised train operation schedule), demonstrating a posture of intensified competitiveness characteristic of private-sector enterprises. This was indeed a *modus operandi* diametrically opposed to managed safety. As if that were not problematic enough, even after it had been confirmed that an accident had happened, incredibly, employees went ahead with scheduled intra-company team-on-team golf and bowling competitions. One of the passengers in one of the ill-fated coaches happened to be a train operator on his way to work. He survived the accident, and, bafflingly enough, instead of joining the rescue personnel who had arrived, he reported to his work place as usual and went about his work. It was only after the company had received word from the Ministry of Land, Infrastructure, Transport and Tourism that it began to install the ATS-P (Automatic Train Stop-Pattern) system (which is designed to automatically decelerate trains running at speeds exceeding a set limit) This sort of corporate behavior shakes to the core the peace of mind that we daily assume with respect to the transportation service.

We take for granted the convenience of the service, including safety and peace of mind, which we purchase for a given price. It commonly happens that the train may arrive after some delay. Most railway companies would explain over the public announcement system the reason for the delay. The chief reasons given are operation-related technical problems or delay in passengers' boarding or getting off the train. These actions speak to a basic attitude of not operating the train until safety has been confirmed. Passengers, for their part, are expected to remind themselves that they put up with the delay for the sake of safety and accept it with grace.

JR, which is answerable to the accident in question, is a "universal service which delivers day-to-day stability and peace of mind" to all corners of the land. It is hoped that JR will re-build its operation so that consumers can ride its trains again with peace of mind and it can reclaim its position as a pace-setter for other private railways services to look up to. "Riding a train scares me" was a comment of one of the surviving victims, which should be appreciated in all sincerity and humility as the voice of someone whose daily lifeline has been disrupted.

KEY POINT

The Lifeline industry differs from other service industries. Every railway company must recognize that it provides safety and peace of mind as integral components of its service.

Recommendations

Japan Railways should:

1. Revamp its crowded train schedule and take into account linkages with other rail services;
2. Give the highest priority to punctuality in its schedule, to the order of seconds;
3. Rescind the punitive practice of generating mental fatigue in the retraining of operators with an accident record.

What Safety Measures and Environmental Policies should Chemical Companies Adopt?

If a chemical company that handles dangerous substances is involved in an accident, it is highly likely that its employees as well as its environment will be greatly impacted. Maximum care must be taken with the operation of chemical processes; it is not enough just to comply with laws and regulations.

In recent years, there have been concerns about environmental contamination by **chemical substances** and their impact on the human body. In particular, contamination by **dioxin** and highly toxic agricultural chemicals, effects of exposure to **environmental hormones**, accidents such as fires and explosions, all pose grave challenges to society. Companies that handle chemical substances are responsible for establishing a thorough-going management system functional in every aspect from research and development to manufacturing, distribution and disposal.

Against this backdrop, the Pollutant Release and Transfer Register (PRTR) was integrated into law in July 1999. Under the law, companies which have cleared a set of criteria such as type of business, number of employees and annually handled an applicable quantity of chemical substances are obligated to manage the quantity of pollutants released to the environment and quantity of transfers. If they are shipping designated chemical substances and products containing them to other companies, they are to provide information on their ingredients and their properties, handling instructions, etc., printed on the data sheet (Material Safety Data Sheet, or MSDS) to demonstrate the safety of the chemical substances in question and issued to the recipient of the shipment.

This means that the community can request the disclosure of data of the companies' individual field offices.

What is noteworthy about the PRTR Act is that it is a legal measure that takes into account the social reality in the context of which "fires and explosions have come to pose challenges to society in a major way."

According to the 2004 *Fire Fighting White Book*, there were 188 fires (including explosions) in 2003, the worst record ever since statistical data began to be recorded. The year 2003 is, in particular, remembered for its string of industrial disasters including fires and other accidents at the petrochemical complexes of some of Japan's representative oil companies. Many human lives were lost and much material damage sustained, leaving the impression that there seems to be an increasingly pronounced tendency for production activities involving chemical substances to become riskier.

ISO 14001 — Environmental Management System (EMS), published in 1996, provides a remarkably useful environmental protection guideline. It provides a set of international standard specifications applicable to the building of a continually operational system supporting the improvement of **environmental performance** such as alleviation of the environmental burdens of organizational activities, products and services. Unlike the PRTR Act, it is not equipped with legally binding power. One may consider it as a trademark of the industry's pro-environment effort.

Provisions for **accident prevention** are incorporated in the intent of program implementation of the EMS. When compliance with the PRTR Act and acquisition of EMS certification become dominant in corporate culture, chemical companies will be investigating the causes for environment-impacting accidents, resulting in a higher possibility of accident prevention. It will in fact be an ideal accident prevention system with a **double-check system** geared to prevent accidents.

A study by this author reveals that the enactment of the PRTR Act was followed by a rapid rise in the number of EMS certifications. This shows how chemical companies reacted very sensitively to the issue of environment preservation through the short period preceding and following the enactment of the PRTR Act. Upon expiration of the "PRTR familiarization" period in May 2001, however, a slowdown in the rate of EMS certification acquisitions set in.

According to *Numbers of Privately Managed Places of Business Classified (at Semi-Detailed Level) by Type of Industrial Enterprise (7 Types) and Employees Broken Down by Gender for the Whole Nation for Fiscal 2001* compiled by the Statistics Bureau of the Ministry of Internal Affairs and Communications, factories, field offices and mining stations under the heading "Chemical Industry" numbered 5,908 as of 2001. Of them, only about one-fifth were EMS-certified companies. The chemical industry continues to be in a situation in which further refinement of the corporate communication process for crisis management (consciousness) purposes is hoped for.

KEY POINT

Companies that handle dangerous substances must develop a process that offers society "safety" and "peace of mind" by not only complying with the law, but also pro-actively building a self-governing environment management setup in an exemplary manner.

Recommendations

1. Industry must not only practice managerial activity based on legal restrictions, but also have in place safety-maximizing and environment-preserving measures that are firmly based on specialists' and their own internal guidelines.
2. The community should actively request individual local branches of pertinent companies to disclose their data (pertaining to quantity of chemicals released and status quo of management of quantities of transferred substances).

How to Deal with Asbestos Damage

Society has become increasingly sensitized to the damage caused by asbestos which is used in building materials. Japan has lagged far behind Western countries in working out restriction policies and modalities of victim relief through collaborative work between government and industry.

Asbestos damage is developing into a serious social issue. As a result of coverage by various news organizations, society's interest has been aroused, and the Japanese government has begun to propose measures of legal redress for victims and develop replacement materials. Japan has only now begun to formulate emergency redress schemes after having lagged so noticeably behind Western countries.

Asbestos is a mineral fiber known in Japan as *sekimen* (lit. "red cotton") or *ishiwata* (lit. "stone cotton"). Constituted of fine fibers 1 to 2 microns thick, they float in the atmosphere in bundles or singly. The effects of asbestos on coalminers and factory workers are now well-known. Those who inhale asbestos dust continuously over long periods, in time develop asbestos in the lung, lung cancer and malignant mesothelioma. Many asbestos-containing building materials are integrated in cement slabs and other formative materials as fixed ingredients and, unless cut by saw or drill, are rather unlikely to contaminate the interior of rooms. The problem is that builders did not take measures ensuring sufficient safety at their construction sites where dangerous construction materials were being used, and the government was slow in reacting with emergency measures to introduce restrictions on the use of such construction materials. By 2008, the Government had announced a policy to completely ban asbestos use, but as of today not much is happening with respect to the relief of the victims. The drafting of the victim relief bill continues to be stymied (as of August 2005) because of disagreements over how to determine the scope of the affected/victimized population, method of certification, financial resource allocation, etc. By contrast, Germany was relatively quick in implementing thoughtful redress measures.

In 1972 Hauptverband der gewerblichen Berufsgenossenschaften (Central Committee of the Trade Union), which manages a public workmen's accident compensation insurance system for cases that occur within Germany, opened a center charged with the task of collecting data on workers in danger of having been exposed to asbestos. So far, the center has on file records of the state of health of approximately 270,000 patients and urges those in highly dangerous conditions to be diagnosed; every year, more than 40,000 patients try out early treatments.

With regard to use restrictions, asbestos air blasting was banned in 1979; asbestos was designated as a dangerous substance, its use effectively put on hold, in 1990; and its use was categorically banned in 1993. Germany's swift action in responding to the issue must surely reflect the German society's unrelenting, fine-tuned reaction to the issue.

Generally speaking, when it comes to environment-conscious production activity, government and people on the one hand, and industry on the other, are in opposite positions. The former desires a production mode that will bring the least possible burden to humanity and the community, while the latter desires a mode of production that brings the least possible burden to its business. As a result, the latter, though conscience-stricken, will adopt a format that yields a higher production efficiency based on what will burden the environment.

In Germany, there was a convergence of interests between government, industry and people when it came to environmental policy. At an early stage, the government announced an all-encompassing economic law, and the people were given an arena for powerfully voicing their opinions on environmental policy. The ruling party, armed with a battery of strict environment-related laws on its side, strongly pressured industry. Industrial houses, for their part, continued to uphold a conscious self-admonition by inviting members of environmental protection organizations as external board members. In short, all the social elements opted for an **environment-conforming action**.

There is a clear difference between adopting redress measures following damage verification and having a response mechanism in place decades in advance. In the case of the former, a completed socio-economic system must first be undone before it can be rewoven, which would presuppose extra time for conducting studies on the replacing system and retooling the legal machine, which in turn would make for certain difficulties in securing the necessary financial resources.

KEY POINT

The government, people and industry are seldom unified over environmental policy.

Recommendations

1. There should be a reciprocal monitoring system for positive airing of government's, industry's and people's environment policy study.
2. Society must work for further progress in environmental education.

Case **94**

How Intellectual Property Infringement is Spreading

Cases of infringement of the intellectual properties of Japanese corporations are increasing at a rapid rate. This problem concerns not only the victimized corporation but also the theft of the technology assets of Japan.

In June 2004, the Act for Establishment of the Intellectual Property High Court was enacted, whereupon the Intellectual Property High Court ("IPHC") was duly installed, and the court officially commenced to function in April 2005. The stage for this chain of events had been set at the initiative of, among others, the Intellectual Property Promotion Conference, a consultative body to the Koizumi Administration (as of October 2005), which called for the installment of a judicial organ dedicated to the infringements of intellectual properties detrimental to Japanese corporations.

IPHC is vested with the same authority as the regular high court. If the civil cases being fought over patent rights or utility model rights are of a substance that concerns LSI design or program authorship, IPHC has jurisdiction over all hearings of immediate appeal.

As for appeal hearings concerning intellectual properties such as design rights, trademark rights, authorship neighboring rights, etc.,

IPHC will hear cases filed within the jurisdiction of the Tokyo High Court.

In the area of administrative litigation, when a person in disagreement with a decision in an intellectual properties case files an appeal against the Patent Agency, the first trial will be handled by IPHC.

According to a report of the Intellectual Properties Issues Committee of Transdisciplinary Federation of Science and Technology, of the intellectual properties cases in which Japanese corporations were the plaintiffs, 276 have been filed against Japanese corporations, 41 against American corporations, 34 against European corporations and 94 against Asian corporations.

Especially problematic are damages caused by China in the form of imitations and pirated versions. The damages for 2001 are claimed to total ¥2.2 trillion to 2.8 trillion, with the number of cases of trademark, patent and utility model infringements rapidly on the increase.

Infringements of intellectual properties of Japanese corporations centering on damages caused by imitation products are so overwhelming that taking legal action and waiting for the courts' decisions no longer makes sense. Infringements perpetrated in foreign countries need to be addressed and countered promptly at the level of the central government.

KEY POINT

Endeavors by corporations can go only so far toward protecting their intellectual properties.

Recommendations

1. Everyone should start learning from the elementary school level how important it is to protect our intellectual properties.
2. IPHC should aggressively hire more specialists (legal staff with a background in advanced technology studies).
3. The authorities should secure a larger budget to cover intellectual property litigations.

Case 95

How to Secure Food Safety and Information Reliability

Food safety must be backed by reliable information and safety systems, if food scares are not to become little more than a charade staged by government and big business.

Cases including the mad-cow incident have happened in succession, rattling food safety to its core. Against this backdrop, consumers' concerns have been aroused regarding the **traceability** of products to their production history.

Traceability provides the mechanism for shedding light on who used what feed to raise cattle or, further downstream, fertilize agricultural produce so as to manage and trace the distribution history of produce. It is a system that will promptly provide all relevant information of the process from produce production to distribution. With the enactment of the Beef Traceability Act of December 2003, some 4.5 million cows being raised in Japan began to be managed by a database of individually identified cattle. As the first trial in the world, IC chips are used to contain information under the **traceability system**.

This system, however, brings with it a number of assorted issues: massive social cost toward readying it for implementation at the operational level, infeasibility of completely securing food safety even after the system goes into operation, uncertainty as to how to secure the reliability of information, etc. Of particular urgency is the need to secure **food safety** and the **reliability of the information that the food is safe.**

The traceability system serves the purpose of verifying the history of production and distribution, and *not* of guaranteeing food safety itself. Some supermarkets, reportedly, use personal computers in their food department to make it possible, by punching in the cow ear tag number, to trace the place of origin, producer's name and address as well as "BSE inspected", "meat and powdered bone not used" and other entries.

What is the basis for our trust? Be it food safety or information reliability, without third-party certification by a neutral organization, as exemplified by the ISO series which provides quality control, guidelines for businesses, or for environmental communication management, any endeavor to address the issue will prove meaningless.

KEY POINT

Any latest system introduced is bound to end up as an act of self-justification by the corporation unless it solves the fundamental issues of safety and reliability.

Recommendations

1. When a food traceability system is to be introduced, participation by all businesses in the transaction chain is indispensable.
2. The system should have as its centerpiece the guarantee of a third-party certification organization in order to secure food safety and information reliability.

How the Natural Sciences, Arts and Social Sciences Can Collaborate

The causes of natural disasters and the multi-layered fashion in which they impact society engender a host of problems which cannot be resolved with the help of measures endorsed by only one field of learning. If the effects of a disaster are to be alleviated, interdisciplinary cooperation is indispensable.

One of the authors has recently (in August 2008) become actively associated with the Transdisciplinary Federation of Science and Technology (an umbrella non-profit organization that houses societies of arts and social sciences and natural science lineages). As a member of the Conference that meets in the fall, I attend many meetings with scholars from diverse specialized fields to discuss the ideal mode of existence of the various fields of learning and the need for the fusion of different specialized fields. At one meeting, the topic arose of a need for **fostering a relationship of collaboration and interlinked work between natural sciences, arts and social sciences** toward alleviating the effects of natural disasters.

It is the disciplines of the natural sciences (geophysics, etc.) that take charge of investigating the causes of natural disasters and acquiring measurement, while the disciplines of social engineering (architectural engineering, etc.) and social sciences (economics, etc.)

handle damage estimation. Social psychologists and other profession in related fields, working with government agencies and the media, engage in communicating disaster information to society in universally understandable terms as well as formulating proposed methods of restoring soundness to disaster-stricken communities.

The study of history is to learn from the past and pass the lessons on to future generations. Linking the two fields of natural science and social psychology will help towards this end.

Tamotsu Igarashi (Japan Aerospace Exploration Agency (JAXA)), who is developing a natural disaster observation and measurement technology, is deeply involved in the building of such an interdisciplinary linkage. "We must at all times be thinking of how to put to good use the disaster observation information acquired from satellites," he says, "and the providers of science and technology, I believe, will have to clarify how cost-effective the service will be for society, the consumers of such information. There is an ongoing query as to how much damage can be prevented by warnings issued on the basis of observation data, and whether loss of human lives and property can be prevented at all..." This can be understood as a call to social scientists for the establishment of a firm collaborative relationship.

To see to it that the data obtained from strenuous exertions in observation work will not be wasted in the interest of serving society, researchers in the social sciences must strive to develop their day-to-day work as well as maintain close working ties and collaborative relationships with researchers in the natural sciences and related fields.

KEY POINT

A multi-dimensional approach comprising diverse specialized fields is required in the study of how to deal with the effects of natural disasters.

Recommendations

1. In the study of natural disasters, the humanities and the sciences should aggressively organize interdisciplinary forays and conferences in the spirit of harmonious collaboration.
2. Public institutions such as universities as well as private sector organisation that conduct natural disaster research should pro-actively employ not only natural science researchers (geophysicists in particular), but researchers in the social sciences as well.

Case 97

How to Make Your Investor Relations Work

Audited statements of accounts or announcements of financial information no longer provide the yardstick for measuring the soundness and potential growth of corporate activities.

The concept of **investor relations** ("IR" hereafter) is attracting attention as the latest publicity to keep investors in corporations informed.

According to the Japan Investor Relations Association (JIRA), IR is defined as "the corporation's activity of disclosing as appropriate and offering on an ongoing basis, for the benefit of shareholders and investors, corporate information which they may need in making investment-related judgments." It is claimed that IR activity will make it possible for shareholders and investors to collect information efficiently, and that corporations, for their part, will earn on the capital market an appropriate evaluation which will serve them in their financial strategizing, including raising of funds. As a recent trend, IR information is increasingly carried on corporations' websites. There are more and more cases of corporations disclosing through websites pertinent information to shareholders and institutional investors, as the occasion warrants it, as real-time publicity.

As IR activity is being promoted in Japan with ever greater importance attached to it, corporations' fund-raising sources have shifted from banks to securities markets, and strong demand has grown for greater fairness and transparency of the securities markets reflecting the growth of the ratio of shares of overseas institutional investors through the 1960s and the 1970s. IR is said to trace its origin to the United States, where, in the 1950s and 1960s, annual reports began to be published to counter exacting audits which imposed heavily on corporations. Japanese corporations, who are under no illusions about American institutional investors who have nurtured trust in the IR system over many years, appear certain to aggressively promote an increasingly active use of this system.

Investors rely on the financial status and growth potential as well as the medium- and long-term strategic thinking of corporations for their investments, but it is difficult to judge such data if the only information available is information made public during the closing of accounts or trends in shares gyrations. Share prices go up and down after corporate decisions are made, and audited statements of accounts and financial statements are no more and no less than what they are: after-the-fact reports on business activities. What the investor wants to know is in what direction the corporation intends to steer itself in the future and what is on the mind of its management.

IR is also considered to provide an important arena for the corporation to pro-actively make public any irregularities and accidents, alongside its financial information. The investor often examines the corporation's financial health as well as its commitment to discharging its social responsibilities to use the information as one of his investment decision-making tools. IR should be actively utilized as a window for **airing irregularities and accidents in real time**.

It is important to make websites and IR the main tools of raising operating funds as well as maintaining real-time dialogue with investors on an ongoing basis.

KEY POINT

Investors estimate the value of a corporation from all points of view.

Recommendations

1. All businesses must comply with legal bindings. (Commercial Code, Securities and Exchange Law, etc.)
2. Additionally, they should continue to represent and describe, from all sorts of perspectives, the value of their corporation (the soundness of its financial condition, its strategic creativity, the status quo of its practice of discharging social responsibility).

Case 98

What are the Consequences of Irresponsible Media Coverage?

Media practitioners should treat their coverage of accidents carefully and accurately. If any case that requires a highly professional cause-and-effect investigation and clarification is mishandled, it will stir up a hornet's nest of social unrest.

On 10 September 2001, Japan confirmed its first case of a cow that had contracted the mad cow disease (bovine spongiform encephalopathy or BSE).

Mad cow disease was first reported in the U.K. in 1986, and is caused by an abnormal protein cluster, a "prion," which causes the cow's brain to sustain spongy degeneration resulting in motor disorder and other nerve conditions. Its incubation period is said to be two to eight years; infected cows die within two weeks to six months after the onset of the disease. Furthermore, it is thought that the infection spreads among the cattle population via ingestion of feeds containing the brain and spinal cord of BSE-infected cows.

Some point out that, if humans contract the disease, it may develop into a new "variant Creutzfeldt-Jakob disease" (vCJD or nvCJD) which causes, as in the case of cattle, sponge-like transformation of the brain leading to difficulty in walking or dementia. As of today, however, no cause-and-effect relationship between the mad-cow disease and variant Creutzfeldt-Jakob disease has been established on a pathologically satisfactory basis.

The Japanese government responded swiftly to BSE. A month and a half after the discovery of the infected cow, the Ministry of Agriculture, Forestry and Fisheries moved to issue a "request that the shipment of 30-month-old or older cows be refrained from," announced a "policy of an across-the-board ban on the import of meat and bone meal products," and other measures, while the Ministry made known its intention to "examine all 30-month-old or older cows for BSE." More Central Government-level security measures were launched in quick succession.

Riding piggyback on the developments, the media engaged in **over-reporting** BSE-related stories, showering general consumers with incendiary stories that would only trigger social unrest. Another side-of-the-coin of the whole episode would suggest that the government had over-reacted which resulted in stirring up social unrest regarding beef consumption.

One point that needs to be heeded here is that it is only *suspected*, and not been definitively established, that eating BSE-infected beef may cause the consumer to develop symptoms of variant Creutzfeldt-Jakob disease.

Despite the fact that no cause-and-effect relationship has been scientifically established in this controversy, the media has blanketed the waking hours of consumers to give the impression that the truth is being disseminated, the cattle industry and retailers have sustained severe damages and the public has been seized by misgivings over a protracted period of time. Can you blame the people for saying that the media "got away with irresponsible gossip mongering"?

KEY POINT

Pulling a scoop on a newsworthy development such as an accident is not the same as stirring up social unrest.

Recommendations

1. The media and other news organizations should enlist the help of a team of specialists when handling a highly specialized case.
2. The media and other news organizations, when handling a case in which news exerts a significant impact on society, should sufficiently verify the accuracy of their reports through a long-term engagement of a team of specialists.

How to Prevent Personal Information Leakage

We hear much today about the "law-abiding nature" of corporations, but, before accepting their stance at face value, we should take a step back for another look at the potentially problematic nature of giant business firms as it relates to corporate management.

Since the recent enactment of the Act on the Private Information Protection, we see corporations in the private sector drafting and making public **Privacy Protection Policy** statements. Everywhere from Internet websites to the monitors of convenience store cash registers, we are made aware of how sensitized business operations have become to the treatment of personal information. This phenomenon can be interpreted as pointing to a corporate act of publicizing to society how businesses are protecting the personal information that crosses their paths.

The Personal Information Protection Act was originally submitted in 2003 as an ordinance in the context of instituting a personal information protection system. The Act comprises five laws, Nos. 57–61, and is formally titled *Five Laws Pertaining to Personal Information Protection* and covers such areas as duties of the Central Government as well as local public entities, measures concerning the protection of personal information and duties of business operators who handle personal information. The requirements of the provisions and guide-lines in question boil down to the following six points (H. Okamura and M. Suzuki 2005; *What You Should At Least Know About Personal Information Protection* (*Koredake wa shitte-okitai kojinjoho hogo*). Nihon Keizai Shimbun-Sha):

1. As much as possible, identify in advance the purpose of utiliza-tion, and use the personal information only within the limits necessary for attaining the purpose of its utilization.
2. Acquire all personal information in a proper manner, and, at the time of its acquisition, notify the person concerned, and make known the purpose of its utilization.
3. Try to keep the contents of the personal data accurate and updated; have security management measures in place; and supervise employees and entrusted parties.
4. Personal information may not be handed out to a third party without prior consent of the person concerned.
5. The purpose of utilization and other information with respect to the personal data in the custody of its handler must be accessible to the person concerned; said data must be disclosed, amended, made unavailable for utilization, etc. at the request of the person concerned.
6. Efforts must be made to address complaints, and a response setup must be put in place toward such an end.

With regard to this law, item 3 above is of particular concern. Cases involving information leaks unintentionally perpetrated by business employees that result in theft and data mishandling by entrusted outside parties, among other things, are seen occurring all too often. This is a matter that questions the ethical soundness of business management more than compliance with laws and regulations.

Examples of theft include a case in which a floppy disk of data concerning the customers of the victim's client plus personal infor-mation about several thousand individuals was stolen. Examples of improper data handling include loss of data storage media (USB flash memory) storing ADSL and other contractual information. Accidents such as referred to above not only concern individuals whose personal information is exposed, but, more pertinently, tend to happen more often than not when instructions and orders of the parent company fail to be correctly communicated to the affiliate company in time of a corporate disaster (explosions, fires, etc.).

KEY POINT

Do not waste time minutely studying the points of compliance listed in laws and regulations; instead, more importantly, focus on and find solutions to those aspects of the process of your day-to-day work that are generating problems.

Recommendations

All companies have to be mindful of the following:

1. If commodity theft and similar incidents occur repeatedly, take a renewed look at why such incidents would occur (background and causes for such occurrences);
2. Re-examine the line of command and instruction from parent to affiliate company.

Case 100

Why the Need for an Informatics Education Towards Problem-Solving

2006 will usher in the first group of young people who have methodically studied informatics into university. Universities now face the need to fundamentally reform their curriculum of informatics disciplines.

We are entering an age when, driven by an awareness of the ongoing shrinkage of the younger generations, private universities nationwide are scrambling to admit applicants. They are dispatching faculty members and staff to workshops organized up and down the country to propagate the bright image of the campuses they represent in an effort to win the hearts and minds of college-bound youths.

Admission applicants are given more than one opportunity to take entrance examinations, and admission opportunities have also been created in varied forms. Admission through the AO (Admissions Office) is becoming a more and more widely established procedure today. The AO's application processing includes, in many cases, a self-recommendation based on the evaluation of the applicant's most diligently pursued activities in his/her high school days or a self-presentation at the entrance examination sitting.

Universities, for their part, find themselves caught up in the very difficult position of having to secure the admission of as many applicants as possible and are working out creative breakthrough measures. It is a self-help endeavor universities are exerting as they face the social trend that is shrinking numbers of the younger generation, in order to deal with an ongoing external change.

In the meantime, problems are beginning to surface within the university system as well. For one, the **direction that computer education** should take for 2006 and beyond. In response to a July 1998 recommendation by the Curriculum Council, schools have decided to use computers more fully in the curriculum and information science-related disciplines have become required high school subjects. Under the new setup, depending on the objective, a choice of different subjects are offered in combination, such as "Information A," "Information B" and "Information C," and the ratio of allocated hours for such classes worked out to the entirety of class hours. The students receive thorough training in subjects of practical utility. Thus, students who have acquired information science methodically in high school will be heading university from 2006.

What is taught in computer science classes during the first and second years in college at present has already been covered in high school. Apart from applications development or networking technology as part of programming practice and other disciplines of specialized nature, the curricula is indistinguishable from offerings of yore — leaving newly enrolled undergraduates with little to look forward to. University management would eventually run aground, opening the way for student departures in the worst-case scenario.

It is said that, in information education, acquiring **information literacy**-supported skills is key. These skills are not the same as computer literacy-supported skills, which consist of familiarity with applications that serve practical purposes. Information literacy-supported skills concern themselves with **logical thinking**, which is an indispensable tool supporting such activities as information collection, analysis, problem location, solution proposal and verification. What this writer has come to be keenly aware of as an educator in information science is that none of the skills just listed comes to meaningful fruition without time duly invested in education. An inquiry which never ceases to be asked of this writer year after year is: "Could you kindly show me what to consider before anything else?"

I would submit that information science in the context of university education should define the computer as a technical means of information collection and processing in support of logical thinking, and set as an objective the training of information literacy skills.

KEY POINT

Stagnant, unrefreshed information education runs the risk of opening the gate for student departures.

Recommendations

1. Universities should teach disciplines geared towards encouraging logical thinking skills and using the computer as a technical assistant.
2. The information education curriculum should be designed to be directly applicable, and linked, to the specialized courses taken by students in their third and fourth years.

Case 101

How Compliance should be Reconsidered: Organizations that Comply with Laws and Regulations While Satisfying Ethical Requirements Considering Autopoietic Theory

The expression "compliance" is used differently in Japan from other countries. If a company is to provide a truly safe service, it should gain an understanding of the concept of compliance as current in other countries and put that concept to practical use.

In promoting its business activities, a company must comply with pertinent laws and regulations laid down by the legislative authorities and operate within the bounds of the stipulated conditions. This basic premise has, of late, come to regain notable relevance. But the concept of compliance and the manner of its application as understood in Japan are different from how they are understood in other countries. Here we will re-look the concept as it is generally understood in Japan, and examine the essential meaning of what the expression is intended to convey.

Situations can occur in which mere compliance with laws and regulations may not suffice. On 5 May 2007, a young woman lost her life in a jet coaster derailment at an amusement park in Osaka. The accident occurred when the alloy axle supporting a pair of wheels broke in half, but the vehicle continued to career forward until the wheels derailed off the track, resulting in the vehicle falling to the ground. The vehicle tilted at a sharp angle, and the passenger very tragically hit her head hard against an iron fence and died instantly. Any organizational problem the amusement park may have had was taken up in sensational media reports, focusing on its less-than-complete safety management setup and sloppy corporate response to the emergency brought about by the accident and other issues that came to light subsequently, all reported in the news in great detail. But this accident cannot be conclusively attributed only to the various problems with safety management at this amusement park. This was a case that led us to assume that the accident could have been averted if compliance with laws and regulations had been practiced along with operational judgment and corporate ethics.

The immediate cause for the accident was the snapping of the alloy axle due to metal fatigue. To avoid accidents from parts snapping, legally prescribed inspection as stipulated in the Building Standards Law must be performed periodically, results of the inspection to be reported to the local authorities concerned, and, as a self-directed action on the part of the company, "flaw inspection" should be performed. Broadly, these two inspections are required. Flaw inspection shoots an ultrasonic wave at a metal part suspected of suffering deterioration for data indicative of how the wave is deflected, or, using magnetic powder, examines patterns that form on the surface of the part in question. Based on the results of these tests, the degree of metal fatigue and other conditions are measured. The problem with this flaw inspection is that it is based on the Japanese Industrial Standards (JIS), which are intended to provide an industrial standard guideline. More specifically, it might be pointed out, compliance with JIS is a "self-directed action" (a matter of corporate ethics), taken voluntarily and not a legally binding requirement.

The amusement park in question was operating in a terrible situation in which managerial behavior on which human lives depended would be allowed to be taken as a function of individual companies' self-direction and ethical standards. The authorities quickly moved to announce that it was going to make flaw inspection mandatory through explicitly stated provisions in the Building Standards Law Enforcement Rules to clarify the legal definition of flaw inspection. The relevant legal instruments which will in due course be put in place by the competent authorities and the industry's guidelines should be considered in an interlocking context.

Compliance management in the corporate context is best understood as comprising, from the conceptual standpoint, two specific aspects: (1) the act of complying with laws and regulations, and (2) the act of abiding by corporate ethics, managerial ideals, etc. General debate on the subject of compliance management in Japan is for the most part predicated on (1), but may also embrace the practice of managerial ethics when the ideal-based practice of some countries is looked to for reference. It is not a permissible interpretation of compliance management, in deploying business activity, to assume that a company is free to compete based on market fundamentalism so long as its behavior stays within the bounds of the laws and regulations laid down by the authorities. The company must set forth a standard of behavior for itself and assiduously adhere to the faithful practice of its ethics-based standard of behavior. We must reconfirm the meaning of the very term "compliance." If the true meaning of the word had been understood deeply and a behavior based on it practiced as a corporate act, an awful fatal accident such as described above might not have happened. What is important here is how to establish the framework for the adherence by and practice of corporate ethics.

In setting in motion a managerial ethics adherence regime, the first agenda item is said to be the appointment of a "Managerial Ethics Coordinator," or a "Managerial Ethics Officer," whose duties will include provision of concrete guidance or consultation in matters pertaining to the in-house practice of managerial ethics. It will also be his, or her, responsibility to call the attention of the Ethics Committee or the management executive board to any instance of inadequacy of any department's response/reaction to any development in light of the company's ethics guideline or any pertinent laws and regulations. Furthermore, an organizational setup proposal has been submitted that calls for the officers to periodically report any management ethics issues to the Ethics Committee and, in collaboration with the legal affairs department and the audit department, discuss and elaborate the means of resolving outstanding issues.

The point is that an independent, responsible unit (at personal as well as departmental levels) should be instituted, charged with the task of discharging an auditor-like function with respect to corporate business operations from an objective perspective. One method is to create independent units with the purpose of causing goals to be attained and streamlining such units so that, through their independent functions, the integrity of the entire organization can be maintained. These streamlined units will form a new system, which is completely separate from the system responsible for the conduct of day-to-day business, and the significance of this will lie in the fact that it will independently cause work to be performed.

And recently there has been some interest in autopoietic theory as a new approach to business ethics. "Keeping ethical and moral condition is much the same as radiating autopoietic power and this is the power of organizational growth" (Araragi and Kono *et al.*, 2007). To explain autopoiesis briefly, it means "self-reproduction". When this concept is applied to organizational behavior, this is translated as "self-reference" and "self-purification". To practice ethical organizational behavior it is necessary to revitalize the communication process and make it a continuous one. Both organization design and consideration of the nature of communication are equally important.

KEY POINT

If safe services are to be provided, it is necessary for industry, business organizations and authorities to work closely together to nurture a shared consciousness toward an ongoing securing of safety.

Recommendations

1. A company must sort out instances of potential danger that have been encountered and identified in the course of its day-to-day work, and on an ongoing basis keep working on an operational system that can provide a means of responding quickly to danger-fraught situations when they do occur.
2. Industrial organizations must not only comply with all relevant laws and regulations laid down by the authorities, but also design and promote their own industry guidelines.
3. The authorities must dedicate their attention to flexibly amending and applying relevant laws and regulations over which they have jurisdiction.

Note: The present case study is a substantially modified version of the article entitled "Compliance Reconsidered: Organizations That Comply with Laws and Regulations While Satisfying Ethical Requirements," (2005), *Postal Services Research Institute Review — Special Issue on Intranets*, pp. 15–17. Corporate Development Department, Japan Post.

Epilogue

One year has passed since the Chuetsu Earthquake in Niigata Prefecture on 23 October 2004. The earthquake claimed 51 lives and left some 4,800 wounded. As of this writing (5 November 2005), there are still more than 9,000 people confined to temporary dwellings at evacuee centers. At the joint memorial service, which was widely covered by the media, the heads of concerned local municipalities pledged as early an area recovery and activity support as possible. One particularly exalting scene occurred when a boy, still not quite past his years of innocence, rose to powerfully offer a prayer that "the story of the tragic experience of a natural disaster be told and retold through all future generations." This event was an eloquent testimony to the community's heart-rending sorrow, but it also looked forward with hope and joy to the coming generations.

The year 2005 marked the first anniversary of the Chuetsu Earthquake of Niigata Prefecture, the tenth anniversary of the Great Hanshin-Awaji Earthquake and the 60th anniversary of the end of World War II, all milestones in the passage of time and each denoting a significant experience of unspeakable woe. Rather than question whether such woes were caused by natural or man-made disasters, should we not direct our attention to the fact that, each time one generation replaces another, people allow their fear to blind them to the very dangers that threaten to bring on loss of human lives and of properties?

Long after the disasters, people in communities that have lost relatives and those close to them will continue to live with the memories of those departed souls and with the hurt of this misfortune etched deeply in their hearts. It is a fact, at the same time that, as time goes by, people tend to bury and consider lost the various woes experienced as fragments of the phenomenon of history. The lapse of time mercilessly leaves in its wake a fear that people are being robbed of their ability to assemble together an art of risk management to support disaster prevention and alleviation efforts to fend off the dangers assaulting their daily lives.

According to German sociologist Ulrich Beck, we must draw a clear line between a culturally and politically perceived danger and an actual existing and expanding danger. He further postulates that it is consciousness that determines the existence of a dangerous situation. For the purposes of this book, we may be allowed to interpret these words as parallel to stating, "Irrespective of whether it is a natural or man-made disaster that is in question, what determines the safety of an individual's existence is whether or not he, or she, has a heightened sensitivity to information and is in a mentally awakened state." What is required of us at this point is to maintain an ongoing sense of fear and keep working on a risk management plan. People are urged to at least develop and uphold, deep in their consciousness, a willingness to prepare for and enough grit to courageously face up to a crisis.

* * *

The text of this book was first used in a "Risk-Ridden Society Studies" class in the Department of Information and Communication at Meiji University. When a case study on the Chuetsu Earthquake of Niigata Prefecture was taken up as the subject matter, a number of students submitted comments. To quote some: "It is expected that non-governmental organizations and non-profit organizations will provide support to help the victims recover from their sense of loss" (Momoko Nakamura, Momoko Seki), "It is also important to make use of the mobility of disaster support volunteers and Self-Defense Forces personnel to lend out learning tools and teach people how to make pertinent judgments" (Mayu Yamaguchi), "Only when the original, pre-disaster condition is restored can recovery be considered to have been achieved" (Yukari Yasumuro), "I was thinking of the flashlight as a portable item for securing a light source if struck with a disaster" (Satomi Hayashi), "I wonder if portable phone disaster victim bulletin boards are easy enough for older people to use, too?" (Kotaro Tajima, Kazuyuki Tamura), and "Compared to the Southern Hyogo Prefecture Earthquake situation, I believe the personal information of victims of the Chuetsu Earthquake in Niigata Prefecture was handled with greater care" (Hiroshi Yamabe). Each of these comments indicates a high level of crisis management consciousness on the part of the students. These thoughts account for only a small portion of the students taking courses dealing with this subject matter.

The students did not regard the horror of the natural disaster being reported by the various media as a case of a safely distant "fire on the other side of the river"; rather they perceived the event as a real-life phenomenon and set about to ferret out any overlooked problem or unaddressed issue so that an effective solution could be identified to provide social assistance and tap into technology-backed assistance methodology. These students are described as having engaged in uninterrupted reflections of a sense of crisis as a *whole-body experience*. They did not satisfy themselves with knowledge acquisition in classrooms only; they found it a moving and significant experience by which they developed a sharply calibrated sense of danger in daily living for which maintaining preparedness and awareness was required.

Those who preceded us and the generation shouldering the core of society today have discharged their important roles in building the foundation for a safety-securing system in society. It is strongly hoped that the upcoming generation, the protagonists of tomorrow, will, in a spirit symbolically demonstrated by that budding young soul in his prayer at the joint memorial service for the victims of the Chuetsu Earthquake in Niigata Prefecture, take over the safety system soundly structured by their predecessors. They will need to search for and transmit to future generations methods of foreseeing or actually experiencing crises that may surprise society so that disastrous effects can be effectively minimized or avoided altogether. We have great expectations for a social culture that favors peace of mind and safety to be maintained so that the society in which we live will not be exposed to natural as well as man-made disasters.

* * *

In the writing of this book, the present author has received much generous help from the various parties concerned. I am deeply indebted to Mr. Tetsuya Kimura and Mr. Yuichi Miyakawa of the Terrorism Prevention Division of the Ministry of Foreign Affairs of Japan for the data, information and other assistance provided in connection with my description of anti-terrorism measures. I would like to thank Mr. Tamotsu Igarashi of the Japan Aerospace Exploration Agency (JAXA) for his perspective on disaster prevention and disaster alleviation through collaboration between the natural and the social sciences.

I am especially beholden to Professor Emeritus Akira Ishikawa of Aoyama Gakuin University, co-author of this book, for checking my manuscript with infinite patience while respecting the purpose of the publication of this book and for the countless words of much appreciated wisdom and invaluable suggestions. Allow me this opportunity to apologize for my inopportune impositions in taking advantage of his generosity toward me and hereby express my most heartfelt gratitude.

My cordial thanks are also due to Representative Director Mamoru Miura and Managing Director Yukiko Ishibashi of Shumpusha Publishing Co., who provided me with the original motivation toward writing the book and to Mr. Toshinobu Nagata of the same company who ably took charge of the task of seeing this project through to press.

Lastly, I dedicate a special expression of thanks to all those who, each in his or her way, provided support for this project but whose names, for lack of space, does not allow me to list.

Atsushi Tsujimoto
November 2005

References

(1995). Crisis Management Industry: Emergency Distribution from Seven-Eleven Japan. *Nikkei Business Daily*, January 30, p. 2.

(1995). It is of Utmost Importance to Arrange Enough Telephone Lines. *Yomiuri Shimbun*, May 30, p. 18.

(1995). More than One-Half of the Respondents Have Not Been Prepared. *Nippon Keizai Shimbun*, August 30, p. 14.

(1995). *Nikkei Sangyo Shimbun (Nikkei Industrial Journal)*, January 24 and 30.

(1995). Risk Management Financial Report. *Nikkan Kogyo Shimbun (Business & Technology Daily News)*.

(1995). Strengthening Disaster-Proof Functions For Every School. *Nippon Keizai Shimbun*, August 23, p. 34.

(1995). *The Asahi Shimbun*, August 24.

(1997). Do Not Forget Valuable Lessons. *Yomiuri Shimbun*, July 17, p. 8.

(2003). Economic Report, Kawaguchi City, December 2003, p. 56.

(2003). Survey on Telecommunication Utilization. http://www.soumu.go.jp/s-news/2004/pdf/040414_1_a.pdf (retrieved July 18, 2005).

(2004). All Mainstay Lines of NTT-East Couldn't Be Used. NTT-docomo Has a Problem To Be Solved, Securing People the Base Power Station. *ITPro*. http://itpro.nikkeibp.co.jp/free/NCC/NEWS/20041101/152015 (retrieved July 27, 2005).

(2004). The Lessons That Were Shown by Disaster-Stricken Area in Niigata Prefecture Chuetsu Earthquake, "Telecommunications that were not broken down". *ITPro*. http://itpro.nikkeibp.co.jp/free/ITPro/OPINION/20041113/152537/index2.shtml (retrieved July 27, 2005).

(2005). A Living God. Study Group of Inamura-no-Hi. http://www.inamuranohi. jp/ (retrieved August 29, 2005).

(2005). About IR, Japan Investor Relations Associations. https://www.jira.or.jp/ (retrieved September 1, 2005).

(2005). About Yokkaichi-City's action on Fires in Petrochemical Complex Attributed to The Tokachi-oki Earthquake. *Yokkaichi-City.* http://www3. city.yokkaichi.mie.jp/WEB1.nsf/0/8d955fcc1b7836c149256db700254 44d?OpenDocument, (retrieved September 25, 2005).

(2005). Can We Get Reparation From Bank? *Yomiuri Weekly,* March 6.

(2005). Hazard Map. rescuenow.net, Vol. 59. http://www. rescuenow.net/ one_point/59_hazardmap.html (retrieved August 29, 2005).

(2005). Japan Information Processing Development Corporation, ISMS Promotion Office, Compatibility Test System on Information Security Management System (ISMS). http://www.isms.jsms.jipdec.jp/ (retrieved July 21, 2005).

(2005). Koshino Kuni Zukuri Hot Hokuriku, The Special Feature on Niigata Prefecture Chuetsu Earthquake in 2004. *Niigata Prefecture, Sightseeing section.* http://210.131.8.6/kyoku/10-23jishin/kensho/01.html (retrieved July 24, 2005).

(2005). Koshino Kuni Zukuri Hot Hokuriku, The Special Feature on Niigata Prefecture Chuetsu Earthquake in 2004. *Niigata Prefecture, Sightseeing section.* http://210.131.8.6/kyoku/10-23jishin/kensho/03.html (retrieved July 28, 2005).

(2005). Koshino Kuni Zukuri Hot Hokuriku, The Special Feature on Niigata Prefecture Chuetsu Earthquake in 2004. *Niigata Prefecture, Sightseeing section.* http://210.131.8.6/kyoku/10-23jishin/shiten/03.html (retrieved July 28, 2005).

(2005). London Blasts: It was a Matter of Life and Death Harmful to Many Citizens. *Hotwired Japan.* http://hotwired.goo.ne.jp/news/culture/story/ 20050708202.html (retrieved July 25, 2005).

(2005). *Mainichi Shinbun,* August 2.

(2005). *Newton,* March, pp. 50–51. Newton Press.

(2005). Pay Attention to Phishing Fraud. *All About.* http://allabout.co.jp/ computer/netsecurity/closeup/CU20040426A/ (retrieved July 19, 2005).

(2005). Phishing. *e-words.* http://e-words.jp/w/E38395E382A3E38383E382 B7E383B3E382B0.html (retrieved July 19, 2005).

(2005). Redressing the Asbestos Damage by New Legislation for Residents, Government's Plan. *Asahi.com.* http://www.asahi.com/special/asbestos/ TKY200508250377.html (retrieved August 30, 2005).

(2005). Report by the Committee of Intellectual Property Problem, Transdisciplinary Federation of Science and Technology, March, p. 5.

(2005). Supporting Substitutes of Asbestos, Ministry of Economy, Trade and Industry Submitting a Draft on a Rough Estimate of the Cost. *Asahi.com.* http://www.asahi.com/special/asbestos/TKY200508250378.html (retrieved August 30, 2005).

(2005). The Bills on Privatization of Postal Services Administration were Passed in Plenary Session of the House of Representatives. *Yomiuri Online.* http://www.yomiuri.co.jp/atmoney/news/20050705mh16.htm (retrieved July 24, 2005).

(2005). The Threats of Nature. *Tokunosuke.* http://tokunosuke.client.jp/think61.html (retrieved August 29, 2005).

(2005). Today's Term: Intellectual Property High Court. *Nikkei Electronics.* http://techon.nikkeibp.co.jp/NE/word/050511.html (retrieved July 24, 2005).

(2005). Yahoo Auctions. http://auctions.yahoo.co.jp/ (retrieved July 18, 2005).

(2007). *Yomiuri Online,* May 5–26. http://www.yomiuri.co.jp.

(2008). Sankei News (http://sankei.jp.msn.com/), November 11.

(2008). Searchina News (http://news.searchina.ne.jp/), September 4.

(2008). *Yomiuri Shimbun (The Daily Yomiuri),* May 15.

Araragi and Kono *et al.* (2007). *Psychology of Organization Injustice.* Japan: Keio University Press. p. 6.

Arano, K (1995). *108 Lessons from a Magnitude-7 Earthquake.* Japan: Shogakukan.

Bureau of Social Welfare and Public Health, Tokyo Metropolitan Government (2005). Architecture and Hygiene of Water, Guiding Principles on Indoor Conditions' Maintenance and Control Concerning Sprayed Asbestos. http://www.fukushihoken.metro.tokyo.jp/kankyo/bldg/asbestos.html (retrieved August 30, 2005).

Disaster Prevention System Institute (2005). Tank Fires Occurring Successively, Doubted Morals and Revising a Law. http://www.bo-sai.co.jp/tankkasai.htm (retrieved September 25, 2005).

Fire and Disaster Management Agency (1995). *Hints for Earthquake Disaster Preventions.* Japan: Printing Bureau of Ministry of Finance.

Hadfield, P (1995). *Sixty Seconds That Will Change The World.* Diamond Inc.

Hiroi, O (2003). Social Influence and Measures on Mad-Cow Disease Occurring in 2001. *Research Survey Reports in Media, Information and Society,* No. 19, March 2003, pp. 232–264. Institute of Socio-Information and Communication Studies, University of Tokyo.

Hiroi, O (2005). Local Residents' Behavior and Communication of Disaster in Downpour on Niigata Prefecture and Fukushima Prefecture in July 2004. *Research Survey Reports in Information Studies,* No. 23, pp.164–165, 227, 247. University of Tokyo.

Ishikawa, A (1985). *Qualifications of International Business Professionals To Be Desired.* Japan: Doubunkan. pp. 49–50.

Ishikawa, A and Tsujimoto, A (2006). *Risk and Crisis Management 99.* Shumpusha Publishing, pp. 87–88.

Japan Information Leak Control Management (2005). The Report on Measures Against Skimming Crime. http://www.jilcom.or.jp/skimmingreport1.html (retrieved July 20, 2005).

Katagata, Z (2005). Introduction to New Office System (25), Information Security Management. *Bukka Shiryou,* March 2005, pp. 13–15. Construction Research Institute.

Kojima, H (2005). What's PAYOFF? http://www.remus.dti.ne.jp/~laputa/zatta/pay_off/payoff.html (retrieved July 24, 2005).

KPMG Business Assurance (2003). *Compliance Management,* Touyou-keizai-shinpousha, p. 13.

Map Editing Department (2009). *Map to Help You Get Home in Time of an Earthquake Disaster — Capital District Edition.* Japan: Shobunsha.

Ministry of Foreign Affairs, Japan. *Q&A: Measures Against Terrorist Explosions For Japanese/Japanese Corporations in the Process of Going International,* pp. 11–12.

Ministry of Land, Infrastructure, Transport and Tourism (2005). The Damage Situation of Sightseeing Spot Caused by Sumatra Earthquake and Indian Ocean Tsunami, Official Announcement of Research Report Made by Group Constituted by Public and Private Investigators. http://www.mlit.go.jp/kasha/kisha05/01/010315_3_.html (retrieved August 29, 2005).

Mizoue, M (1993). *Big Earthquake Hits Tokyo.* Japan: Chukei Publishing Company.

Mizutani, M (2003). *Business Ethics.* Japan: Doubunkan Publishing. p. 129.

Nikkei Business (1995). *Want to Know Crisis Management Now.* Japan: Nikkei Business Publications.

Fire and Disaster Management Agency (2004). *White Paper on Fire and Disaster Management.* http://www.fdma.go.jp/html/hakusho/hl6/h16/index.html (retrieved April 1, 2005).

Noguchi, Y (1995). *Risk Management and Contingency Planning for the Documents.* Japan: Nihon Jitsugyo Publishing.

PHP Institute Office (1995). *Disaster Prevention Manual.*

Sassa, A (2001). *Crisis Management in Natural Disaster: Mitigate Coming Disaster!* pp.17–18. Japan: Gyosei.

Statistics Bureau, Ministry of Internal Affairs and Communications (2001). The Number of Offices and Workers (Man/Woman) in Modest Scale Industry in Japan. http://www.stat.go.jp/data/jigyou/2001/kakuhou/zenkoku/zuhyou/a012.xls (retrieved April 1, 2005).

Tanaka, H (1998). *Compliance Management.* Japan Productivity Center. p. 224.

The Japan Accreditation Board for Conformity Assessment (2005). The Statistic Data on Organizations Which Satisfy ISO 14001. http://www. jab.or.jp/cgi-bin/jab_statistic_14_j.cgi (retrieved April 1, 2005).

Tokio Marine & Nichido Risk Consulting (1995). *Talisman,* Vol. 20.

Tsuge, H (1994). *Newly Revised Survival Bible.* Japan: Hara Publisher.

Tsuge, H (1994). *Survival Bible (New Edition).* Japan: Hara Shobo.

Wadatsumi, K (1995). 850 Symptoms for the Pending Earthquake. *Yomiuri Weekly,* March 12, pp. 27–29.

Planning Exercises and Q&As

The following planning exercises and Q&As concern some of the issues and cases discussed in the main body of this book. You will have to invest some time in the exercises, all of which concern important issues that must be discussed and resolved at individual, household and organizational levels. The Q&As, on the other hand, are designed to test the depth of your understanding after a reading of the text, which contains the keys and hints. The authors would be gratified if this exercise would provide the foundation for an actual problem-solving experience and help you deepen your risk and crisis management consciousness.

PLANNING EXERCISES

Exercise 1   Create a disaster prevention map. The disaster prevention map will include disaster prevention measures in your home, emergency exit route, route to evacuee gathering point, method of communication in an emergency and communication relay points.

Exercise 2   When a tsunami warning is issued, how are you to handle the evacuation of sick people, old people and babies to safety? Explain in specific detail.

Exercise 3   Suppose that an earthquake of magnitude 7 or greater has just struck when you are at home, at your work place, in transit to your work place or on your way home, in a conference hall attending a meeting, etc. Think through what would be the best action for you to take, and compile a plan of action.

Exercise 4   For each of the following two scenarios of an earthquake-stricken situation, work out a homeward transit (evacuation) assistance facilities map:

1. From school or work place (starting point) to your house (destination)
2. From school or work place (starting point) to the nearest wide-area coverage evacuation open space (destination)

Point to keep in mind: Pencil in your routes on a store-bought map. As much detailed as space allows, write in detailed information on homeward transit (evacuation) assistance facilities and other useful spots (such as filling stations, convenience stores, watering places, "home-bound commuter support stations" designated by local public entities [prefectures, municipalities, etc.]).
Note: It will be useful, in writing in these notations, to refer for ideas to informative materials prepared by the Disaster Prevention Committees of the Prefectural and municipal offices concerned, regional disaster prevention plans and related materials, etc.

Exercise 5   Textbooks for elementary school education (for Japanese, social studies and science) sometimes include topics dealing with disasters (such as *The Straw Torch* discussed under Case 19: How a disaster can be turned into a lesson). Search relevant sources for episodes concerning disasters and recount the lessons learned from them.

Exercise 6　In frequently flood-afflicted areas, you will more often than not come across monuments that record in specific detail such disaster-related data as flood water level, and extent and other aspects of damage sustained. Closely study cases described on such monuments; prepare a schematic drawing of estimated damage-affected area(s) based on an assumption of a flood on a similar scale occurring today; and calculate the extent in monetary terms of resulting physical damage incurred mainly to residential structures. (It would be ideal, as part of the work, if you compare the flood damage amount [as assessed at the time of the flood described on the monument] against an estimated damage amount for the assumed flood.)

Exercise 7　Make a list of items to pack when an emergency develops (emergency provisions, water, portable radio, household medicines, etc.). Consider and decide how to sort them out, and what means (backpack, traveling bag, etc.) to carry them in.

Exercise 8　Try NTT's "emergency messaging service", and report on its usefulness.
Note: This system is to serve the purpose of retrieving information concerning the safety of family and close circles at the time of an earthquake disaster. Dial "171" without a prefix, and you will be able to use "Disaster Message Relay Dial" (connection possible also from a portable telephone). On the first of every month, and throughout the Disaster Prevention Week (August 30–September 5 every year), the system is open round the clock. A call fee will be charged.
　As regards "disaster message boards on the portable telephone," NTT DoCoMo, au, TU-KA Cellular and Vodafone operate personal safety confirmation systems, which allow you to access confirmed information via

personal computers or portable telephones simply by registering your name with the portable telephone company you subscribe to. Ask your telephone company for further details.

Reference Materials (regarding Exercise 8): *Metropolis of Tokyo Public Information* (Vol 717, p.1) compiled by Public Information Section, Bureau of Citizens and Cultural Affairs, Tokyo Metropolitan Government.

Q&As

Question 1	Name two things you must take care of, as much as time permits, when attempting an exit from your house or work place because an earthquake or fire has occurred.
Answer	Go to *pp. 109 and 191.*
Question 2	What are the three important points to bear in mind regarding what you should be wearing in an emergency or when escaping a disaster?
Answer	Go to *p. 123.*
Question 3	When sending for an ambulance, what information should you provide, and in what order?
Answer	Go to *p. 33.*
Question 4	Explain what tsunami information is.
Answer	Go to *p. 21.*
Question 5	Immediately following the outbreak of a disaster, there is a limit to what the government can do. What organizations' offer of help will it become necessary to accept?
Answer	Go to *p. 11.*
Question 6	If you become involved in a war when traveling overseas, what action should you take?
Answer	Go to *p. 75.*

Question 7	Explain what "typhoon psychology" is.
Answer	Go to *p. 97*.
Question 8	Explain the external as well as internal factors of the outbreak of a fire.
Answer	Go to *p. 107*.
Question 9	What are the four criteria of judgment of a crisis?
Answer	Go to *p. 158*.
Question 10	The outbreak of a major earthquake disaster renders the use of wire-carried communication lines (connection with another party) difficult. Explain why this is so.
Answer	Go to *p. 5*.
Question 11	Explain how to deal with the demagoguery that surfaces following the outbreak of a disaster.
Answer	Go to *p. 35*.
Question 12	Explain what "rumor-generated damage" is.
Answer	Go to *p. 43*.
Question 13	What method is available to avoid becoming a victim in a bomb incident?
Answer	Go to *p. 81*.
Question 14	What measure(s) should one take to avoid victimization by phishing fraud?
Answer	Go to *p. 135*.
Question 15	What is a hazard map?
Answer	Go to *p. 156*.
Question 16	Explain what technical issues are holding up the food traceability system at the present time.
Answer	Go to *p. 217*.
Question 17	Which agency, or organization, should assume the initiative toward resolving the issue of infringement of a corporation's intellectual property?
Answer	Go to *p. 215*.

Question 18   Explain what action was taken by the government, industry and people of Germany toward compliance for environmental protection.

Answer   Go to *p. 213.*

Question 19   The purpose of the environment protection measures and safety assurance measures taken by facilities that handle dangerous substances (corporations) can be met through compliance with the PRTR Act, but additionally there are International Standard Organization specifications which should ideally be considered and complied with. Explain such specifications.

Answer   Go to *p. 210.*

Question 20   What is meant by measure of defense against the payoff?

Answer   Go to *p. 121.*

Question 21   Corporate network damage can lead to the elaboration of a new management strategy. Explain why.

Answer   Go to *p. 202.*

Question 22   When surprised by an earthquake while overseas, which should you first consider, self-help, mutual help, or public assistance?

Answer   Go to *p. 127.*

Question 23   What is the most typical single cause for the occurrence of leaks of clients' personal information in a corporate setting?

Answer   Go to *p. 228.*

Question 24   Explain what measures you should take in order not to become a victim of credit card-related damage.

Answer   Go to *p. 138.*

Question 25	Explain what limitations there are to disaster recognition (application of the Assistance Act) in an earthquake disaster.
Answer	Go to *p. 50*.

Question 26	Generally speaking, communication lines in a disaster-stricken situation are apt to get jammed, making it a challenge to establish a connection with the party you wish to contact. At the time of the Chuetsu Earthquake of Niigata Prefecture, however, there was one communication line that remained open. Think of what three communication routes may have been in place.
Answer	Go to *p. 46*.

Question 27	In alleviating the after-effects of, and preventing, natural disasters, collaborative work between natural sciences, arts and social sciences is indispensable. What is meant by "division of labor" between the two fields as applied to earthquake prediction and control of post-tremor confusion?
Answer	Go to *p. 219*.

Question 28	When torrential rain falls, should an evacuation advisory and evacuation instruction be provided even when there is a possibility of being spared a disaster?
Answer	Go to *p. 52*.

Question 29	Explain what sort of mental preparation a lifeline company should have in place.
Answer	Go to *p. 205*.

Question 30	What are the points to verify when you utilize an Internet auction?
Answer	Go to *p. 134*.

Question 31   What procedures should you implement before using free software that can be acquired on the Internet?

Answer   Go to *p. 130.*

Question 32   We live in the Internet Age. Explain what IR (investor relations) activities are expected from the public relations department of a corporation.

Answer   Go to *p. 222.*

Question 33   With the contents of Case 80: How to Counter Weaknesses in Supply Chain Management in mind, summarize the direct as well as indirect losses that would be incurred if a jet on a flight training mission crashed, disrupting a high-voltage power transmission line.

Answer   Go to *p. 181.*

Index